Secrets of the Capsule Wardrobe:

How to Find Your Personal Style & Create a Happy, Confident Closet!

By Sarah Eliza Louderback

Table of Contents:

Beauty
begins the moment
you decide
to be yourself

-Coco Chanel

via Devastate Boredom

Chapter 1 – Minimalist fashion - why bother??

Since you're here and reading this, you're at least a teeny bit interested in whittling down your closet and moving towards a minimalist, capsule system. But you still might be asking yourself… can I commit to this? It seems so radical… Is it really worth it?

It SO is.

I promise. It's worth it. It's worth the hassle! It's worth going counter-social and bucking our consumerist "buy more, more, MORE" culture; it's worth learning a new way to think about your clothing; and it's worth making some hard choices. Oh yeah, and it's worth all the counting… and we will be doing a LOT of counting.

But if you don't want to take my word for it, here are three reasons why "converting" to minimalist fashion and/or a Capsule Wardrobe is worth it.

Reason 1 - Less stuff on the planet = a better future for our planet.

Yep, that's a picture of a dump. In a book about fashion… edgy, right?

But seriously, if you like the idea of your great-grandchildren knowing what a tree is, and walking around on the face of the planet without being vaporized by the lack of an ozone layer (don't quote me on that part, ha, I'm no scientist) then minimalist fashion is DEFINITELY your style. And if you are glaring resentfully at this page and muttering, "I donate my old clothing… they go to the needy!" then I have some bad news… even if you donate clothing, it's not necessarily benefitting the underprivileged. According to research recently done by fashionista.com, only about 20% of donated clothing ends up being resold in the US. Another chunk is sold abroad (often wreaking havoc on local economies), another even bigger chunk is "recycled," and another chunk ends up…. you guessed it… in the landfill. In 2014, 11% of donations made to Goodwill ended up carted to the dump — about 22 million pounds worth of goods. Ugh!

So, all that to say, while donating your old clothing is indeed better than tossing it directly into the landfill, it is much more effective to *limit* how much we buy in the first place. That's just logical, right? Pat yourself on the back… by reading this book you've just taken your first step towards a greener world.

A Capsule Wardrobe will help SAVE the PLANET!

Reason 2 - Increased confidence in your own skin.

If you love how you look, you're going to feel more confident. It's as simple as that. And let's be honest, can you really love a closet full of stuff you've half forgotten? Think about the clothes you love.

(I'll wait)

Most likely, a few specific items of clothing came to mind. Maybe they were outfits you wore in the distant younger and/or skinnier past, and maybe they're things you're wearing this very moment, but I'd be very surprised if you visualized fifty different pieces of clothing… or even twenty.

Want to know what I thought of when I did this exercise? I remembered the Barbie sweatshirt I owned when I was eight (and wore until I was twelve, or thirteen, or something wayyy too old…) and a striped maxi dress / black shirt combo I currently own. I LOVED that sweatshirt, because it was comfy and child-me felt cute in it. I love that maxi outfit, because it's flattering and attractive, and I feel good when I wear it. I feel confident that I look like an individual in it (no cookie-cutters here, right?), and I feel *myself*. **That is, fundamentally, the point of fashion — to give you an outlet for self-expression, and to help you feel confident and at-ease in your own skin.**

I'd be very surprised if even a quarter of what is in your closet right now succeeds in that. To think of it a different way — a lot of your clothes are mooching off you, taking up space in your closet without paying "rent" in the form of happiness and utility. The longer something has sat folded in a drawer or dangling from a hanger WITHOUT being useful or bringing you joy, the more back-rent that thing owes you. It's time to evict that lazy wardrobe, friend!

A Capsule Wardrobe will help you feel confident and embrace yourself.

Reason 3 - Eliminating a daily task-based decision is good for your brain.

Lately lots of researchers have been investigating decision making, and self-control, and they've discovered some interesting ways that the two intersect.

To sum up their findings in five words — **decision-making depletes self-control.** If you spend a lot of thought and effort on "finding" an outfit to wear one morning, you're going to have less mental capacity left for focus later that day.

Here's a line from a 2008 Scientific American article on the subject that I found particularly compelling —

"the mere act of making a selection may deplete executive resources."

In other words, the fact that you have to focus on getting dressed as a *task*, and make *choices* about what to wear and whether things "go together," leaves your brain less able to act creatively and decisively for the rest of the day.

Personally, I already struggle to focus due to ADHD… I'm not interested in expending mental energy unnecessarily. And since I now have a Capsule Wardrobe, I don't have to! As I will say later in this book, with my minimalist closet, all I have to do is reach in, pick a base, pick a top, put both on my body, and voila! I'm put-together and ready for the day.

It really is that easy.

A Capsule Wardrobe will allow you more available brain-power to be creative and decisive throughout the day.

FASHION IS

art

AND YOU ARE THE

canvas.

-Velvet Paper

via Devastate Boredom

Chapter 2 – Beginning this exciting fashion journey!

It's okay if you're not ready to commit quite yet. Go step-by-step with me, and you can adapt the concepts I share to meet your own needs. And maybe you'll work into it little by little... After all, it took me a while to make the Capsule Wardrobe commitment myself. Here's what my own journey looked like... I suspect we'll have at least a few things in common, even if your fashion sense and history are a lot different than mine!

That awesome childhood Barbie sweatshirt aside, my own "style sense" was never particularly self-assured, and I accumulated clothing haphazardly for years... a sale here, some thrift-store shopping there, a few gifts to top things off. In college I fell into a group of friends who dressed... well... *eclectically* — and after a while I started picking my outfits based on that group-identity. I loved being recognizable as one of "them" based on how I looked... our main trademarks being vintage clothing and garish colors paired seemingly at random. On any given day I might have been sporting four different primary colors (tights, skirt, sweater and scarf), or I might have looked like a 1930s librarian... in a non-sexy way. It was a fun time of fashion experimentation, but I often chose my clothing based on the group's taste rather than my own. I wasn't aware that that was what I was doing, however, since I didn't have a firm concept of what my own style even was at that point! After I graduated from college, that group identity was no longer part of my day-to-day life, and its influence over my fashion choices began to wear off. I hung on to my college acquisitions, since that clothing still held happy associations for me, but a good bit of my wardrobe became less and less relevant, and less and less frequently worn.

What did remain, however, as I moved into post-college life, was a dread of looking "boring." I didn't want to just blend into the crowd, but I wasn't sure what my personal fashion identity was... cue more clothing accumulation as I dabbled in different "looks" and took advantage of whatever sales I stumbled across. My closet was becoming quite crowded, but I had a hard time knowing how to combine pieces when there were so few cohesive themes among them. When I was in a rush — and when are we all NOT in a rush? — I defaulted to t-shirts and jeans.

And then I discovered Pinterest.

Don't laugh! As an image-based search engine with a social-media component, Pinterest helped me discover the Way of Fashion — mix-and-matching, layering, French style, and (drumroll please!!)... the concepts of both minimalism and the Capsule Wardrobe.

I was fascinated.

Could a smaller, minimalist wardrobe actually make it *easier* to mix-and-match the items in my closet? Could a Capsule Wardrobe eliminate the "I have nothing to wear!" paralysis that afflicted me morning after morning?

I was especially inspired by the idea of a "happy" closet - one that would make me feel comfortable and confident because it was entirely made up of clothes I loved. Isn't it sad that loving my clothes wouldn't be a given? That so much closet space is often taken up by clothes we don't even *like*?

Slowly I began to take baby-steps towards developing a Capsule Wardrobe myself, but a lot of the advice I was finding felt impractical. I definitely didn't have the budget to buy a whole new closet, and many of the bloggers and magazine articles I was reading seemed to take it for granted that my style was the same as theirs, or that the logic behind the clothing choices they were touting as a "capsule wardrobe" would be clear to me. A lot of times, I didn't see any logic behind their capsule wardrobe choices at all. What made those particular twenty things a "capsule"? How could I see past the fashion choices I didn't love, to be inspired to create *my own* minimalist collection of clothing?

It felt like there were SECRETS to making a capsule wardrobe, secrets that these bloggers and magazine articles weren't keen on sharing with me...

And there kind of were!

So, mid-way through my journey to creating a Capsule Wardrobe, I started a fashion series on my blog, Devastate Boredom, entitled "How to Create a Capsule Wardrobe Without Losing Your Mind!" Please note — though I was only mid-way on my journey, I thought I had already arrived. I had made a lot of progress, yes, but establishing a minimalist, Capsule Wardrobe IS tricky, and I still had a lot of learning to do before I would be ready to write this book.

You might be wondering... why IS the process of shifting our wardrobe habits so very tricky? Based on my own experience, I think its partially due to the fact that we often don't know ourselves as well as we think. We *think* we like blazers, but in fact we almost never wear them. We *think* we need to own a wide variety of colors, but in reality we tend to reach for that particularly rich shade of green whenever it's clean. We *think* we know ourselves, but we're actually on autopilot, going off of assumptions that are frequently no longer true... and maybe never were.

The other part of what makes issues of clothing tricky is that our closets are often near-and-dear to our hearts. Our wardrobes quickly accumulate associations with memories and with moods, and even can reflect psychological hang-ups and anxieties. When we decide to change the way we dress, we often end up having to work through all of that baggage along the way. But I will say it again — it's so worth it! The result of taking ownership over your style choices and being deliberate in curating your clothing collection is a life of greater freedom and intention.

And then, of course, there *are* secrets to creating a Capsule Wardrobe! When I began that blog style series that would later give birth to this book, I was still in the process of figuring all of them out. I didn't even understand the importance of balanced bases until I wrote a blog post exploring the idea, and that concept is truly one of the Top Secret cornerstones of a successful Capsule Wardrobe. It was a long journey for me, but I'm so glad I kept at it — exploring ideas, figuring out how to know myself well enough to discover my style, and working through the anxieties I had allowed to weigh down my wardrobe. I'm glad not only for my own sake, but because it brought us to this moment in time, book in hand, ready to show you the path to a happier closet of your own!

Thank you for joining me here, friend! I'm just a "regular" woman like you — not a fashion designer or a beauty editor for *Vogue*. But I've figured out the logic behind creating a Capsule Wardrobe, and the secrets to making a minimalist style work, and I'm going to break them down step-by-step and walk you through the process.

Because I'm tired of those designers and beauty editors making the rest of us feel inadequate.

And because I'm tired of the fashion industry yanking us around, telling us we have to dance to their tune each season to be beautiful.

You are already uniquely beautiful!

You deserve to feel at-ease in your own skin!

And you are capable of discovering your own style, one that makes you feel confident and that frees you to be your best in all areas of life. You don't have to live with the constant distraction of "what should I wear today?" and "does this look good on me?" any longer!

With a Capsule Wardrobe, you're going to KNOW
what to wear, and you're going to look amazing!

In order to be
IRREPLACABLE
one must always be

different.

– COCO CHANEL

via Devastate Boredom

Chapter 3 — How to find your uniquely gorgeous personal style

So, where do we start in our quest for a happy closet?

Going from our fast-fashion, cluttered-closet, shopping-as-a-hobby culture to a minimalist Capsule Wardrobe is a pretty seismic shift. I better start by explaining how I define the phrase "minimalist Capsule Wardrobe," so we'll all be on the same page going forward.

A minimalist Capsule Wardrobe is a curated collection of clothing you love, that you can mix-and-match almost exclusively. Nearly all your "tops" should pair effortlessly with nearly all your "bottoms," allowing you to own LESS clothing, while maximizing the number of possible outfits.

I love the phrase "curated collection" because it really highlights the deliberation that should go into your clothing purchases from now on. A museum curator carefully considers both the existing collection owned by the museum, and how a new acquisition might add or detract from it. The goal for any addition to the collection is to enhance and expand it, while fitting in seamlessly. The curator isn't trying to own *all* of the art, or to keep up with *every* trend in the art world… there is a vision for the collection, and it speaks to everyone who views it as a result. This is exactly the perspective we need to have as we begin to shape our happy, confident wardrobes!

With the goal of a curated collection in mind, the very first thing we need to do is to figure out YOUR style. Throughout this book I will talk about my own style as an example, but I don't expect my "look" to necessarily resonate with you. That's okay! In fact, that's a good thing... I would feel awkward if you and I were carbon copies. Think of my fashion sense as simply an illustration to help you visualize your own, unique style. In Chapter 10 I will provide you with some actual illustrations as well, of example Capsule Wardrobes in various "looks" — but these are for inspirational purposes only, and are not meant to be prescriptive. I would never dare "tell you" what your style is or should be... that's something you're about to figure out for yourself.

Steps Towards Determining YOUR Unique Style!

Step 1: Recognize that you want your own wardrobe, not somebody else's.

A friend of mine recently told me how she had found a pair of shoes she really liked, at a price she liked even better, but that she didn't get them because she knew someone else who already owned that exact style. Deep down, we all have a strong desire to be unique! That's why I hate the "15 Staples of EVERY Wardrobe" type magazine articles... because the things I "need" to own are going to be different than the things *you* "need" to own. This is due to the fact that we each have different occupations and environments, as well as different ideas of comfort. Even more to the point, what I wear to feel confident is probably quite different than what you do!

Step 2: Decide what you like to wear.

I already mentioned Pinterest, and it can be such a fun tool for exploring fashion and identifying patterns in what you find appealing! However, Pinterest can also suck you into a confusing abyss of "oh that's so pretty... and this is so cute too... and oh my gosh, that dress is the best yet," so while this is a good time to go pursue any fashion boards you might already have created, I'm going to give you a warning to take with you…

Just because something looks good doesn't mean you want to own and wear it.

Shift your perspective to realize that you can admire something, and find it visually satisfying, without wanting to claim it as part of your identity by putting it on your body. Being more deliberate in curating your clothing collection can be a game-changer in terms of attitude, enjoyment, and confidence!

You may have tons of cute skirt pins on your "Looking Good" board, but if you never wear the skirts you already own, that should be a red flag. Take the time right now to experiment — wear your skirts for the next couple of days, and see how you feel. Do you enjoy them? Are you wondering why you got out of the habit of wearing them regularly, OR are you wondering why you bought them in the first place?

Same with cardigans, or high heels, or anything really — you might love them on other people or on the magazine page, but if you don't enjoy wearing them yourself **then they don't belong in your closet**.

An example -- I love the artsy, dreamy, "boho" look on other people, but what that style communicates isn't actually what I'm interested in saying about myself. Wearing a flowery, filmy top can actually make me feel uneasy, like I'm pretending to be somebody I'm not. That's definitely not a recipe for confidence!

Just like you can admire art at a gallery without necessarily wanting to buy each piece, you can love how something looks on someone else without wanting to wear it yourself. Once you've realized that, you'll be in a much better place for defining your own style!

Step 3: Head to your wardrobe and start sorting!

Go to your closet and count how many items are hanging there. This is just a starting place, so write it down somewhere and move on. Then, go through each item, and pull out your favorite pieces. The no-brainer, obvious favorite items will come out first, and then add a little drama as you decide about the rest by asking yourself, *"Would I bring this with me if I were suddenly to elope with Prince Harry / George Clooney / Eye-Candy-Of-Choice to Europe?" or "If I only had five minutes before my house was going to be invaded by an army of killer ants, which of these would I grab?"*

Never mind that if you were about to be surrounded by an army of killer ants you probably wouldn't bother with packing clothes at all, haha! This is just to help you determine your favorites with a more critical eye.

If you have more clothing stored separately in a dresser, go there next and repeat. Count, add that number to the first number, and then most likely gape in shock at the total. I sure did! Then start pulling out your favorites once more. Your dramatic determination this time might be fueled *by "If I only had a week to live, what outfits would I wear?" or "Which of these would I put on if I knew I was going to run into Usher / Justin Bieber / Eye-Candy-of-Choice on the street today?"*

Step 4: Identify themes amongst your favorite clothing.

Once you've gathered your favorites, look for the themes among them. "Themes" might include styles, colors, brands, comfort factor, etc. Right now, you are determining YOUR personal preferences… the root of what you actually *like*, laying hidden under all those layers of "but it was on sale," and "but my mother always told me I shouldn't wear such-and-such," and "but everyone in the office wears this kind of thing…"

We are looking to answer this deceptively simple question:

What do you *enjoy* wearing?

When I did this experiment myself, I realized I like simple combinations of color and style. I like long silhouettes, clothes with unexpected details, and solid colors. Oh, and stripes. I really, *really* like stripes. I love neutrals (white, grey, black, not big on khaki), and gravitate towards reds and blues. I'm not picky about brands, and I definitely prefer soft and stretchy materials to snug or stiff fits.

Is some of that your style too? Or do you like geometric patterns? Florals? Lace? Button-down blouses? Sweetheart necklines? Specific brands? All this is data you're collecting on yourself. None of the themes you discover in your favorite clothing are ever "bad"! And you do NOT have to justify what you like or don't like, to anyone, ever. You are the queen of this domain!

Step 5 — Group your "favorites" TOGETHER in the closet and/or dresser.

Please do not return your newly-discovered "favorites" to their previous positions, scattered randomly through your closet and dresser! They're going to play a foundational role in shaping your Capsule Wardrobe going forward. For ease of access, cluster them together. Consider hanging the favorites that had previously been folded, so that all of them can be visible at a glance in one specific area of your closet. I'm a big proponent of hanging my clothing… there's a whole chapter on the "whys of hanging things" headed your way later in this book!

Step 6 (optional) — Jot down your findings.

I'm a writer, so it is natural to me to want to record my thoughts and doings. You may enjoy this too, and want to make your discovery about your evolving style more tangible by writing it down in a journal or on a blog. But if it feels like a chore, don't bother!

Whether you write down your style findings or not, be sure to take a moment to bask in the glory — you have now completed your first step towards having a minimal Capsule Wardrobe of your own!

Done with all that? Assuming that you are now tired and/or have other things to do than play with your clothes all day, reward yourself with some chocolate or a glass of wine and take a break! But I have one last assignment for you to do over the next few days…

Wear those favorite outfits! Try to notice if it changes your mood and attitude to be wearing things you enjoy. Does it speed up the morning selection time? Are you able to identify anything new about what makes those items your favorites? Do you suddenly remember why you had gotten out of the habit of wearing that (totally itchy) pink top?

The answers to all those questions will continue to shape your Capsule Wardrobe going forward.

Confident, unique style is in reach for each of us! I'm so excited that you've decided to begin this journey. Together we can curate and organize that closet into a thing of beauty... just like you!

Style is a way to say who you are without having *to SPEAK.*

Rachel Zoe

Chapter 4 – The Winnowing Phase commences!

Yay, you're back! Think about these past few days of wearing "favorites" -- how did it make you feel? Do you have a clearer idea now of the kind of clothing that should go in your happy closet? Keep all of those observations and discoveries in mind as we move forward!

Now that you've made such great headway into determining your style, it's time to eliminate the obvious "chaff" from your wardrobe and come one step closer to a closet that makes you feel confident and joyful. That's right, it's time for… the winnowing phase!

Did you hear a faint, ominous *dun dun DUH* in the background when you read the words "winnowing phase"? Yeah, I heard it too... tackling our messy closets and disheveled sense of style can be overwhelming. It also can be hard to have enough perspective on the items in your closet to know when it is time to part ways with them, but don't worry! I'm here to help!

How does one go about "winnowing"?
(that heading should be read in a Jane-Austen-y tone of voice)

The word "winnow" is an old-timey one (in case you were just pretending to know what it meant a minute ago) and refers to the process by which farmers remove the tasty-edible part of grain from the nasty-straw part, also known as chaff. I like the term because in just one word it explains that we're keeping the good stuff while strategically eliminating the blah / yuck part (that's the technical term there, obviously) so that we don't get a mouthful of straw when we take a bite out of our proverbial wardrobe. Haha!

So yeah, I COULD have said, "it's time for the go-through-your-wardrobe-and-decide-what-you-don't-want-to-keep phase!" but isn't "winnowing phase" much more nuanced?

You're probably familiar with the standard winnowing technique, often relayed in magazines and organizational books something like this: you go through your clothing and make three piles! One *KEEP*, one *DONATE*, and one *CLEAN / MEND* pile! You've probably heard that basic idea a million times, from your mom, from Oprah, from your neighbor who blogs about organizing her house, etc.

But oh, my friend, that is thinking too small.

My special touch (*bats eyelashes*) is to add in a fourth and fifth category... the *PROBATION* category and the *"well, duh, I'm going to need this"* category.

Now you're intrigued, right?

Before I explain my two trademark winnowing categories, here's an efficient way of dividing it all up, because, honestly, it would be dumb to make them literal piles. That's a great way to make all your clothes a wrinkled mess. Plus, whether it's due to a kid, a cat, or general clumsiness, it's a truth universally acknowledged that items arranged in a pile will inevitably be knocked over! (I'm clearly still feelin' the Jane Austen over here...) And then you're left having to re-do all the work you've already done, because now everything's spread all over the floor. No thank you! So here's what you do, instead of making piles:

- Your *KEEP* items are going to be hung in a designated area in the **back** of your closet. This space is for "favorite" things only! Everything else is going to be fighting it out for the right to stay in your collection.

- Your *PROBATION* items are going to be hung in a second designated area in your closet, but right up **front** this time.
- Your *SELL / DONATE* pile is going to be in an empty box or a paper bag (or three or seven…), ready to load up and ship out.

- Your *CLEAN / MEND* pile is going to be in your laundry basket.

- Your *"well, duh, I'm going to need this"* category of items will end up in whatever clothes-storage-space is most out of the way in your home. This might be a guest room closet, or that annoying drawer that you have to yank extra hard to open. You can decide for yourself about the precise location, after I explain further in a second.

Three simple steps to winnow your closet:

Step 1 - Transfer your previously-determined "favorites" to the back of your closet (i.e., put them in the "*KEEP* section").

You can put your favorites on the backburner for a moment, since for the next few days you'll predominately be wearing clothes out of your *PROBATION* section... which will basically consist of any non-favorites left in your wardrobe at the end of this winnowing process.

Step 2 - Section out *"well duh, I'm going to need that!"* items.

These are the items you might not *enjoy* wearing, but have situational usefulness that will arise eventually. Items in this category will vary depending on your circumstances, but can include:

- *Interview-appropriate clothing.* It's ideal to have 2-3 different outfits, since getting a new job can often involve multiple rounds of interviews and you might not want to wear the exact same blouse to each one!

- *A number of very-dressy wedding- and cocktail-appropriate clothing.* The number you keep depends on your specific stage in life... and what circles you run in, haha! PS if you're friends with the governor or any assorted celebrities, pretty-please invite me to your next party!

- *Specific "work clothing," particularly if your environment requires business attire, business casual, or you have an actual set uniform.* Those things will (obviously) need to stay accessible for the work-week, so keep them sectioned together towards the front of your closet. If it makes sense for your circumstances, you can always create a second, work-appropriate, Capsule Wardrobe, separate from your weekend-wear capsule.

- *Clothing in a smaller size.* IF you are actively working on losing weight, definitely tuck away a few basics and favorites in the next size down. However, as a general rule, don't keep a lot of clothing that is too big or too small for you! Holding on to too-roomy clothing can turn into a self-fulfilling prophecy of gaining weight back, and having to stare at clothes that no longer fit is just depressing. When you get down to those smaller sizes again — and I have full faith that you WILL if that's your goal — you're going to deserve new clothes to reward your self-discipline anyway!

- *Very cold- or warm-weather clothing.* Depending on your environment, very cold- or very warm-weather clothing might only be necessary for a small segment of the year. Get these things out of your day-to-day space! You've going to need them, yes, but they don't need to be mingled in with the rest of your consistently-useful clothing.

- *Heirloom clothing.* I would never suggest you get rid of an heirloom that holds meaning for you. Just move it out of your "regularly scheduled clothing" section of the closet!

- _____. (Fill in the blank with whatever you know you're going to need to wear again in the next year... you know you!)

Do not leave the *"well duh, I'm going to need this"* items scattered in with the rest of your clothing! They are visually cluttering your space, and your goal is to make it easier to find and keep track of the stuff that brings you joy. That's why a guest-room closet can be the perfect place to stash this category; it's all still accessible, but it's out of the way.

Step 3 - Sentence the remaining clothing to *SELL / DONATE* or *PROBATION*.

A quick but important note! While colorful, unique pieces will likely evoke the strongest emotional response, **neutrals and basic pieces are hugely important in a Capsule Wardrobe, serving as the "spine" that holds it all together.** As a general rule, don't get rid of any of them quite yet (unless of course they're stained, don't fit, etc, etc).

For the moment, go ahead and place all neutrals and basics in probation, and we'll come back to them after we've discussed the importance of color choice and balancing your bases in upcoming chapters.

Now go through the rest of your closet, meditating on the questions below.

- **Does this belong to an "old" me?** For myself personally, a lot of my crazy vintage clothing from college fell in this category. I know myself better now, and most of those items simply belonged to an earlier version of myself. However, on the flip side, just because you've had a "favorite" since high school doesn't mean you have to get rid of it… if it still makes you feel happy and confident, you're golden! **Advice:** If there is a sentimental tug keeping you from getting rid of specific items of clothing even though you never wear them anymore, take a quick mirror-shot of you wearing the outfit, and journal or blog about the memories it evokes. After that, let those items go! **It is the memories that are valuable… the rest is just fabric.**

- **Would I buy this again if I saw it in the store today?** Pretend that the item costs a normal amount for you to spend. Would you pay that right now, or would you pass that item by and keep browsing? If you have to admit you wouldn't buy it again, into *DONATE* it goes. If you aren't sure, stick it in *PROBATION*. And if your answer is a resounding yes, you've happened upon a forgotten favorite! Hang it in your *KEEP* section.

- **Does this piece DESERVE to be added to my curated collection of clothing?** Think galleries and museums here, people! Are you wearing this piece out of habit, or does it *deserve* to be in your collection because it brings you joy or makes you feel confident?

Step 4 – Gather any qualifying items into your *CLEAN / MEND* pile as you go through Steps 1-3… then address those items ASAP!

Do I have to explain this category? It includes all stained items and anything with missing buttons, tears, holes, etc. **Give yourself a three-day window to deal with these things, and get rid of them if you haven't cared enough to finish by the deadline**. Yes, it's a short window, but we don't want you to lose momentum, and we *definitely* don't want the pile of CLEAN / MEND to become just another fixture in the corner of your bedroom. That's why we located this category in the laundry basket... you're going to need that laundry basket freed-up before too long, right? RIGHT?

Advice: Don't wash something BEFORE mending it, or it might make small holes morph into big ones. *shakes head ruefully in recollection*

More Advice: The only way I EVER actually manage to mend anything is if I bribe myself by watching a favorite movie, and work while I watch. I recommend that method!

Now go get to it!

Winnow away with enthusiasm, knowing that you are getting closer and closer to your minimal Capsule Wardrobe with every item you eliminate.

Remember, for the next week or two your assignment is to ONLY wear outfits including items from your *PROBATION* section -- do three probationary items layer so beautifully that suddenly the outfit is a favorite? Fantastic! Does wearing an item for the first time in a year remind you that that the elastic is worn out, or that the cut isn't good on you? You know what to do. And if you simply can't make yourself wear some of those *PROBATION* items out into public at all — that's awesome too! You can throw those straight into the *DONATE* bag and never waste your time on them again.

A quick note, in case you're freaking out -- I am not made of money, and I'm not assuming you are either! **It is fine to leave some items in *PROBATION* for right now simply because you can't afford to go out and replace everything at once.** But as you continue to fine-tune your minimalist Capsule Wardrobe, you will be able to start replacing those items with new favorites as time goes by and opportunities (read: sales!) arise.

Okay, true confessions as we wrap up the winnowing phase... how many items of clothing did you count in your closet and dresser when you started this process? How many are left in *FAVORITES* and *PROBATION* now? And how many items of clothing are now headed for a better life via donation?

Keep refining your style collection over the next few days or weeks as you wear your probationary clothing and decide how you *really* feel about each item... the following chapters on color choice and balancing your bases should also help you to eliminate a good number of things pretty easily.

I'm excited for you! You're already SO much closer to achieving the organized, happy closet of your dreams!

The soul becomes dyed with the color of its thoughts.

-Marcus Aurelius

via Devastate Boredom

Chapter 5 – The drastic and undeniable importance of color choice in a Capsule Wardrobe

I recently came across a blogger decrying the idea of having capsule wardrobe as too "overwhelming" with all of that "mixing and matching." While I totally understand that no one system will work for everyone, I have to say…

If your Capsule Wardrobe is overwhelming, you're probably doing it wrong!

When you DO have a Capsule Wardrobe, you can literally pick a base, pick a top, put them on, and look great. Boom, you're done. There is no hassle about mix-and-matching once your wardrobe is set up... it all just WORKS, no thinking required.

BUT to have a Capsule Wardrobe that works this smoothly, there is one drastically, undeniably important thing you have to commit to now.

looks around nervously

If you really are committed to a minimalist Capsule Wardrobe, you're going to need to limit what colors you own.

watches reader gasp and cringe

Yes, limiting your color choices can be so hard! But for a true Capsule Wardrobe, you want a piece of clothing to look great with as many other pieces as possible.... which basically means you can't own all the colors of the rainbow. It's a sacrifice, but it is a reasonable one given what you will get in return.

Personally speaking, my Capsule Wardrobe consists of black/grey/white (what I call the "family of neutrals"), and the "highlight colors" red, royal blue, and turquoise.

MY CAPSULE COLOR CHOICES

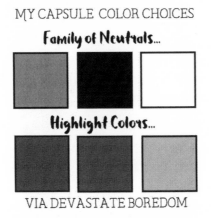

VIA DEVASTATE BOREDOM

Since setting up my closet this way, I can throw on *almost* any top with any bottom, add an accessory or two, and look put-together. Like I said... boom! Five minutes, NO thinking, and I'm done.

It's true! I've even tested it a few times by literally closing my eyes and picking a top and a bottom, and it works. With a few exceptions, I can put on that top and bottom and look good... and even more importantly, feel *confident* in how I look. I can go about my day without the "ugh, oh no, I have nothing to wear" headache, and with my full resources of focus and decision-making still at my disposal. Because remember that study I mentioned in the prologue? Any time you can eliminate "the mere act of making a selection" you can avoid depleting "executive resources." Which means your Capsule Wardrobe can free up more of your brain for being creative and decisive!

Maybe all of those annoying, "no, what do YOU want to eat / watch / do?" exchanges you have with your girlfriends are rooted in the fact that all of you had a terrible time deciding what to wear this morning!

Let's take the plunge and figure out the color choices for your Capsule Wardrobe… it's worth it, I promise!

2 Easy Steps to Choosing Colors for your Capsule Wardrobe:

Step 1 - Start by picking your "family of neutrals," specifically the foundational piece… black, OR brown and/or navy.

Let me start by saying, I do not believe we should abide by mindless, antique Fashion Rules like "don't wear white after Labor Day." Girl, wear white whenever you want, I give you permission! BUT when it comes to mixing brown and black, or black and navy, my own personal opinion is that there was a fashion rule about it because when people wear them together, frequently it looks… accidental. Like that person meant to grab her black blouse, and got ahold of the navy one instead without noticing. Or like she meant to put on the brown shoes, but the lightbulb in the closet was out and she grabbed a black pair instead. On the few occasions I wore brown shoes with a black dress, or a black belt with brown pants, I felt like anyone who happened to notice my outfit was wondering, "did she mean to do that?" …and that worry, inside my own head, detracted from my otherwise fantastic outfit.

Please note that I'm not saying it is impossible for a person to pull off brown and black in the same outfit! I recognize that it is possible, and that person might be you… You rare, beautiful unicorn you!

(I think I borrowed that line from Amy Poehler's *Yes Please…* an awesomely hilarious book, btw!)

HOWEVER, if you're not sure whether you are that rare beautiful unicorn, here's the question you need to ask yourself to figure it out.

Can I wear black shoes with a brown dress (or vice versa) and feel confident?

If your answer is yes, awesome! I admire your rare and beautiful unicorn-y-ness. I know y'all are out there! My blogger buddy Lisa over at Syncopated Mama is one of you wonderfully confident, lucky ladies. Feel free to skip to *Step 2: Pick Your Highlight Colors* with my blessing, 'cuz this next part probably won't apply to you.

However, if your answer was, "no, I don't love how I look when I mix black and brown," than you're now facing your first important color choice of your Capsule Wardrobe.

Which is:

Do you *want* to wear black?

Because, if so, you're ruling out brown and navy for your capsule closet, period, end of story. And, conversely, if you'd rather wear brown or navy, then you've just ruled out including black in your minimalist wardrobe.

You might be rolling your eyes here, and thinking I'm crazy. Why can't you have both in your closet, without *having* to wear them together?

Simply put, it's because you need to be able to maximize and balance your bases. Balancing your bases is one of the foremost secrets of the effective Capsule Wardrobe, and we will discuss in depth in the next chapter. It's also because of all those duplicate-style brown / black / navy shoes, purses, and belts that are jammed into all the nooks and crannies of your closet... oh yes, I know they're there! Just by choosing to have only one foundational neutral color out of those three, you can cut down on all that clutter by as much as 66%!

Look at it like this — if you own six brown shirts that you can't wear with any of your three black bases, you're simply not going to have a functional Capsule Wardrobe. Remember that the whole idea is that you want to be able to mix-and-match *nearly everything*. ALL your bases should be able to be worn with almost all of your tops. You can give yourself a few exceptions, but each exception makes your Capsule Wardrobe more complicated, and less flexible. That's just an unfortunate reality.

And, if you're saying, "Well, these six brown tops go with my khaki and white bases, and these five highlight color tops go with my black bases," then you have essentially created two separate Capsule Wardrobes. This would be completely fine if one was for work and one was for casual wear AND you were careful to store each separately, but otherwise your closet is never going to attain the mindless "shut eyes + pick two items = look great!" ease of a true Capsule Wardrobe.

If you truly want a "real" minimalist Capsule Wardrobe, then you have to pick either / or on the *black* vs *navy / brown* question. And once you do, it has pretty far-reaching ramifications!

As soon as I chose black as the foundation of my color scheme, I was able to get rid of all those brown and navy tops, skirts, pants, purses, shoes, belts, socks, etc, without another thought. It was so freeing! And it was so much stuff! Just that first step made a huge difference in simplifying my closet choices.

After you've picked that pivotal (and perhaps controversial) "foundation color," you can decide for yourself which of the remaining neutrals you want in your "family" — I like grey and white but have never been crazy about tan/khaki, so my finished family of neutrals is black, grey, and white. You want to pick your neutrals with your highlight colors in mind — if your pastel highlight colors don't have enough "va va voom" when paired with white, you might want to leave that one out of your family of neutrals. If you don't like how easily lighter colors show dirt, or don't love how somber the darker neutrals look, you would want to take that type of preference into account as well.

In the end, your family of neutrals could be navy, grey, and tan. Or brown, tan, and white. Or— you get the idea, right? I mean, I *could* list all of the possible combinations, but I'm pretty sure we both have better things to do... so let's go on.

PS If you're still not convinced about why you can't have both black **and** brown / navy in YOUR Capsule Wardrobe — after all it is YOUR wardrobe, good grief why is this writer-person so bossy already? — then I'll admit right now, you're completely right. This is YOUR closet we're talking about. It's up to you to adapt a system that works with your environment and style. My personal opinions on what makes a family of neutrals most effective don't have to be a deal-breaker in your quest for a Capsule Wardrobe. Read on, but know that you can (and should!) decide for yourself in the end. I wouldn't have it any other way!

Step 2 — Pick your highlight colors.

Once you've picked your family of neutrals, then you get to choose two to four compatible colors to build your wardrobe around. You probably identified some favorite colors in Chapter 3 as you were finding your style, so going forward is just a matter of committing to those favorites.

You CAN change your color choices in the future! You aren't stuck with these three colors for all of forever. However, at the same time, in order to maintain a stress-free, effortless Capsule Wardrobe, you will need to be deliberate about color choice when it comes to future purchases. Don't worry, we can talk about that more later.

There are a million combinations of what your finished color palette might look like. Maybe a brown / tan / white family of neutrals, with mint, plum, and salmon as your highlight colors. Or, a navy / grey / white family of neutrals, with yellow, green, and pink accent colors… so many options!

It isn't necessary to pick highlight colors that are all compatible (by that I mean, "look good paired together or mixed up together in a print"), but it will make life simpler if they happen to be.

Color Me Lovely – Your Colors, Your Choice!

A quick note about so-called "rules" around color choice: there are lots of ideas left over from the '80s and '90s about how only certain colors will look good on certain people. Stuff like, "Oh you have a 'warm' complexion, so you should only wear pastels…"

That stuff drives me crazy!

I think those ideas are overly prescriptive (talk about bossy!) and also too focused on the precise color of your skin. Any kind of guideline based on skin tone makes me feel itchy. Unnecessary, at best!

I basically believe you should wear the colors that you feel good in. Sure, if you always get compliments when you wear a certain color, then that probably feels pretty good and you might want to take that into consideration! However, I'm here to say that it is rare to see a color on someone and think, "Gee, that green makes her look terrible."

In fact, I have never thought that about anyone, wearing any color, EVER. In my humble opinion, that's just not how colors work.

Sure, I don't love every color I see, but that judgement (usually along the lines of, "hmmmm, that's a weird green…") is just on the color and not on the person wearing it. I'm also always aware that these "judgements" are subjective, just like my whole conception of beauty is subjective... and that what I find appealing color-wise does not negate the preferences of whoever is wearing the "weird" green. In fact, my opinions have no effect *whatsoever* on that stranger's color preferences, in the same way that her preferences have no bearing on my own color choices. Color preferences and choices are just one small component in the endless collection of choices and preferences that make each of us unique.

And when you come down to it, our conceptions about color are often not even our own. If your mom or grandmother thought bright pink was "too showy," or said you only looked good in dark colors or light colors, then it's likely that you yourself still retain some of those ideas, even if it's just subconsciously. But I have good news! You don't have to continue to be shaped by other people's ideas of beauty, and other people's ideas of what colors are appealing or appropriate. You can be free to choose your style!

For years I thought I was too pasty-pale to wear white, and that I would look "washed out" if I did — but then one day at the mall I took a small risk and tried on a white blouse. Stop the presses! 'Cuz I looked *good* in it. I looked summery and fresh, and not a bit ghost-like. These days I enjoy wearing white regularly... and moreover, whenever I do wear it, I also enjoy the fact that I now feel free to do so. I have renounced a silly rule established by some magazine article I read as a teenager, and that feels good. I make my own style choices now, thank you very much!

The same thing happened to a good friend of mine too. Recently we were chatting about how she had always thought she "couldn't" wear yellow, because at some point when she was growing up her mom had told her it wasn't flattering to her skin tone. When her husband saw her looking at a yellow sweater in a store and encouraged her to buy it, my friend had to deliberately step outside of the fashion-zone her mother had assigned her years before, and try something new. And she looked great! She received several compliments the very first time she wore the sweater out, and better yet, the whole thing helped her to feel a little more at-home in her own skin. See the word "own" in that sentence? It's your own skin…. so OWN IT!

Wear colors that make you feel cheerful and comfortable. There are no rules. If YOU think you look odd in a color, don't wear it. But if you do like a color, take ownership of that and wear it with confidence!

That's all!

Okay checking in… are you freaking out a little bit over there about all the stuff in this chapter? I'm telepathically picking up some frenzied thoughts…

"She says I only can have black OR brown? And I can only pick four non-neutral colors?? Is she crazy? Does she think I'm a nun??"

Luckily, you get to decide whether the Capsule Wardrobe system will work for you or not, but before you close this book and write the whole idea off… think about how nice it would be to reach into your closet or dresser, put on the first two items you touch, and look awesome. Not to sound like a broken record, but… it's so worth it!

I have found that the ease of having a minimalist Capsule Wardrobe FAR outweighs the "bummer" of having fewer colors of clothing. And admit it, don't you mostly gravitate towards your favorite colors anyway? Don't those other, left-over colors mostly just come out to play on laundry day?

This whole limited color-palette thing might be easier than you think.

Happiness
is not a matter
of intensity,
but of *balance,*
order,
rhythm,
and *harmony.*

-Thomas Merton

Chapter 6 - Top secret! Balance those bases!

Admit it… some of you are squinting at that chapter title and wondering what baseball has to do with fashion. Busted! You're hilarious… and no, it's not that kind of bases.

But first, let's take a minute to catch our breath! What a journey we've had so far… Over the last five chapters together you've determined your personal style, rid yourself of all the freeloading clothing items that were living in your closet without getting worn, segmented out the ones that you need to keep but don't use on a regular basis, began wearing "probationary" items in order to determine the fate of each, AND decided what colors to build your wardrobe around. Way to go you!

Now I'm about to reveal one of the top-secret requirements of a Capsule Wardrobe — one of those things that nobody else is telling you! This secret is going to help immensely in fleshing out this "capsule minimalist wardrobe thing" for you, in order to have the most mix-and-match options with the least amount of actual items of clothing. We're not looking for volume here! A crowded closet is NOT our aim.

The secret is…

You have to BALANCE your BASES.

NO, this has nothing to do with baseball! Stop thinking about baseball! "Bases" are (as you might guess once you stop envisioning sports) anything you wear on the "base" of your body or as the "base" of an outfit. Pants, jeans, skirts, and layer-friendly-dresses are all "bases." Most people naturally gravitate towards purchasing multiples of what is essentially the same type of base, which leads to the issue of having lots of clothing, but only a few types of "looks."

In order to have an effective minimal Capsule Wardrobe, you have to have a balanced collection of bases. They can't all look alike, and they can't all be the same color. Which is to say, you can't *just* wear jeans. And if you've got black skinnies AND black leggings AND a black maxi dress AND a black skirt in your closet, get ready, 'cuz I'm talkin' to you!

You're going to need a deliberate, balanced approach to "base" pieces, to provide you with a more flexible collection of looks. If you don't have balanced bases, your Capsule Wardrobe will either be 1) Very Boring or 2) Freakin' Huge, which defeats the purpose of a capsule in the first place. Ideally, you should have roughly equivalent numbers of dresses, skirts, pants, etc, with different silhouettes and colors within each type.

If you're feeling confused and/or annoyed ("What?! Now she wants me to get rid of my black skinny jeans? What madness is this?"), don't worry! We're going to approach balancing your bases step-by-step, just like we have everything else so far.

I suspect that you already have some awesome bases, that will work beautifully in your curated closet. So, what we're going to do from here is to identify those great foundational pieces, eliminate any redundancies, and then strategically *fill in* the gaps in your closet, so you can maximize all those gorgeous things you already own. It will be easier than you think!

Let me share a Highly Scientific Graph with you, to illustrate how this will work. This is the graph I made back when I was first figuring all this out for myself. Nobody is allowed to laugh! I'm quite aware that I'm not an artist, thank you very much. It is the SCIENCE that is important here!

Balancing your bases to double your options!

(A highly scientific graph, by Devastate Boredom)

Awwww, isn't it cute though? I literally drew it on a whim one morning with magic markers. It's safe to say that if I had known it was going to get so much attention I would have spent a leeeetle more time making it... well... symmetrical, anyway! Nobody question why that shirt appears to be shingled like a rooftop, either! Think lace, or... something.

Here's the point of the graph:

If you have 4 pairs of jeans and 2 pairs of shorts in a similar cut/color, each "grouping" still only counts as one base item because the "look" is the same. Trust me, nobody is looking to see if the pair of jeans you have on today is the same brand as the ones you wore yesterday, or taking note that yesterday's jeans had six pockets and today's pair only has four. If your jeans all have a similar tone and cut than it doesn't matter how many different pairs you have, because it's still all the same "look."

By eliminating the redundancies and adding two new items to this scenario (the skirt and the dress), you can go from 11 items of clothing and eight outfits, to 9 items of clothing and sixteen outfits.

You know what that means, right? Stop buying jeans, sistah! It's time to branch out. Think about what base pieces you could add that would provide a whole new look for your existing tops. A pair of bright-colored capris, if you have a lot of neutral-colored tops? A long sleek skirt, if you usually live in shorts? A pair of cozy corduroys in one of your "neutral family" colors that you don't already own? A fabulously comfy UPF/SPF striped maxi, perhaps?

Balancing your bases is the KEY to an effective Capsule Wardrobe.

Here is an updated set of graphs to clarify, in case the "primitive" nature of the first was confusing, or you were too distracted by the hilariously shingled shirt to focus...

IMBALANCED Bases

For the sake of the example, let's say that before deciding you wanted a Capsule Wardrobe, you owned the items above. You had 10 pieces of clothing, combining to a total of 8 outfits, since the four pairs of jeans all provide the same outfit "look," as do the two pairs of black pants. After reading this book and purchasing two new base pieces (and presumably ditching the redundant jeans and extra pair of black pants), you would have 8 pieces of clothing and 16 outfits, as seen here.

BALANCED Bases

I'll give you a moment to ponder all this.

…compelling, right?

You can potentially DOUBLE your outfit possibilities, simply by eliminating redundancies and strategically adding just a few new pieces.

3 Easy Steps Towards Balancing Your Bases

Step 1 - Gather your bases and spread them all out.

Gather ALL of your bases — remember, this includes dresses that can be layered! — and spread them out somewhere they can all be visible at once. Group them the way I did in the Highly Scientific Graph.

Step 2 - Analyze what you see.

Are the groupings of certain styles of skirts / jeans / whatever nearly teetering because they're piled so high? **Your goal is to get rid of the redundancies.** Pick your favorite from among that category, and donate the "just okay" extras.

Could you double your outfit options by adding in a couple of different pairs of neutral-color pants/capris/dresses/whatever? Or, if you already have a good selection of neutrals, would a couple of bright-color, or striped, or patterned bases be the better addition? Of course, keep in mind that the answer to that last question will also depend on the colors of the tops you will be mixing-and-matching!

Write down your analysis. List what bases you have "covered" already, and where you have gaps in your wardrobe that need balancing. Jot down ideas for what colors and styles might fill in those gaps, based on the tops and layering pieces you already own.

Step 3 — Go shopping.

Actually, finish reading this book before you do, because I've got an awesome chapter coming up with rules and guidelines for Capsule Wardrobe shopping!

But after that, take your analysis with you to the mall and balance those bases! **Go shopping for specific things —** black jeans, for example, or even the broader "layering dress in one of my family-of-neutrals colors." Go to that specific section, or department, or rack, and only look for that particular thing. Though of course, if an amazing top in one of your highlight colors jumps out at you, or you happen across a style of base that isn't on your list but could still work nicely to fill a gap, then you have my permission to try those on too. But, as much as possible, try to limit your focus — and your precious decision-making energy — to finding just that one specific thing that you know will help flesh-out your Capsule Wardrobe.

I have two reminders for you as we wrap up this chapter, and though at a glance they might seem to contradict each other, they're both still true just the same! **The first one is to remember to "know thyself" as you're deciding how to approach adding variety to your wardrobe. Balance your bases in ways that fit your style and personality**. Never buy or keep bases (or any item of clothing) just to make the "math" of the Capsule Wardrobe work. If you aren't wearing it, and know quite well deep inside that you never will, donate it or skip the purchase to begin with!

However… if your comfort zone is "yoga-pants-only" or "no-skirts-ever," you will probably find that you will have more fun in the future if you provide yourself with more options. All of what I just said about knowing yourself still applies! But if all the looks in your minimalist closet are too similar then it is very likely you will get bored with them, and constantly find yourself hankering to go shopping to find something new. **Changing things up by adding a different silhouette or two to your Capsule Wardrobe can keep you from getting bored, while increasing your outfit options exponentially.**

So, "know thyself..." but don't take it for granted that you ALREADY know yourself.

You are always growing and changing as an individual! *Keep* getting to know yourself continually, by testing new things out

---

on a regular basis. Who knows… maybe your phobia about wearing shorts stayed behind in college, while you've since "graduated" to a much higher level of body-comfort. Or, like the friend I told you about earlier, maybe you will realize that you actually look great in a color your aunt / grandmother / step-mom always told you to avoid. Keep an open mind regarding how you view yourself, your style, and your clothing, and you might just surprise yourself in exciting ways.

A Capsule Wardrobe is all about simplicity… but simplicity is not code for boring! And to reinforce that concept, here comes a chapter all about learning to mix-and-match your outfits adventurously with joy AND confidence!

As soon as I saw you, I knew an ADVENTURE was going to happen.

-WINNIE THE POOH

via Devastate Boredom

Chapter 7 - Now multiply outfits, adventurously...

Okay, before we start talking about multiplying outfits, I've gotta check in with you... are you still wearing probationary items each day? If you've already worked your way through them and are back to wearing favorites, awesome! But if not, keep plugging away! Remember, if you hate the idea of having to wear a certain probationary item, that's instant proof it belongs in the donation bag. It may be that just the *threat* of having to actually *wear* some of the things stuffed in the back of your closet might be enough to reveal your true feelings about them!

One of our key words on this style journey is "minimal," right? Our goal is to keep whittling down our clothing collections until each piece is maximized and valuable. HOWEVER, we still want to be adventurous with what we wear, so our Capsule Wardrobe doesn't start to bore us. That means finding some clothing combinations that might not be immediately obvious to you.

This chapter is designed to help you prevent a common problem: the formation of limiting habits around how you wear your clothing. At least if you're like me, certain shirts are *always* worn with the same skirts, or certain pants with a particular blouse, or that one dress and sweater... sound familiar?

We want to break these habits. After all, what happens when that one particular skirt is in the wash? You're back to having to THINK about what to wear! *shakes head in horror*. We want to arrive at a place where you can fully embrace the mix-and-match capabilities of your closet.

As a side benefit, this process will probably also help you to eliminate more items from your closet, when you realize that they are simply impractical in a Capsule Wardrobe. You're also likely to come away with a better idea of what items you might add to your capsule in the future, so you'll be prepared when it's time to discuss shopping tips in a few chapters.

There are two ways to explore this "multiplying outfits" idea... an easy one and a more involved one. Pick which you prefer based on the time you have at hand, as well as on how much difficulty you might be having wrapping your brain around the whole "Capsule Wardrobe" concept.

Option 1 - The Eyeball Method

In this version of "multiplying outfits," you spend five or ten minutes each morning for a week or two, eyeballing your closet and randomly pulling out tops and bases, saying, "Whoa, they do work together! This is awesome!" Then you get dressed and go about your day.

If a particular pairing seems to have potential but you're just not entirely sure about it, you can test it with a day's wearing. If you're happy in it, super! If not, you know what to do!

*cough**donate**cough*

But if you're trying the above and saying, "Oh man, I don't know... maybe they work? I'm not sure... this Capsule Wardrobe thing is so hard..." then you might need to invest a little more effort by trying out Option 2.

Option 2 - The Look Book Method

If you have a little more time at your disposal or are feeling insecure about mix-and-matching your wardrobe beyond your established jeans-and-tee or skirt-and-sweater combos, the Look Book Method might be for you.

In this version of "multiplying outfits," you're going to need a camera and/or a pal whose fashion sense is similar to what you're going for.

Including a bestie or a significant other whose fashion sense is *different* from yours is possible, but riskier, since what they "like to see" might not be what you feel good wearing. If you do loop one of these folks in to help you, be sure to clearly describe to them (with photos if possible) the "look" you feel confident wearing, and that you're trying to achieve. Remind them you aren't asking them if they would wear the outfit themselves! You're asking if the two pieces combine well according to the style you enjoy. On second thought, if your significant other is a man, you definitely should NOT include him in this process. All this fashion talk is way too abstract for most dudes to handle!

To test out the mix-and-match capabilities of your evolving Capsule Wardrobe, and figure out which pieces deserve a place in your happy closet, we're now going to have a fashion show... and you're the star!

Cue the catwalk music!

Head back to your closet and pick a base. Try on every single top you own (hopefully that's much fewer by now!) with that base, struttin' it up for your friend to see.

Then do the same thing with another base, and on until you've mixed-and-matched everything in your closet.

Your friend needs to be armed with a camera, and take a full-length photo of you in each outfit you try. If a friend isn't available, use the timer function on a camera to take the photos instead.

Even if you're not interested in making the photos into a Look Book to remind you of outfit possibilities after your catwalk session, still go ahead and take the pictures. It might feel a little silly in the moment, but being able to look back later at all the outfits you tried, seeing them both from a distance and in the context of other cute outfits, will help immensely in deciding what you think about them.

Keep in mind that YOU are the final word on whether or not an outfit "works." Your Style Advisor might not be crazy about a particular pairing, but if *you* love how an outfit looks and makes you feel, it honestly doesn't matter what your friend or spouse says... yours is the opinion that counts!

Your style = your choice.

And as a bonus, the happier and more confident you feel in what you're wearing, the more attractive you actually will appear to others. So, yay for that too!

Remember, this moment in time is all about being adventurous! Try wearing a button-down dress open over a pants outfit, duster-style! Try wearing a long skirt over a shorter dress for a smoothly-tucked look! Try a collared shirt under that sweater, or under / over that dress! Wear skinny jeans under a short dress! Combine different textures and patterns! And so on, in any and all pairings you can imagine.

Don't forget to try different belts and shoes with your catwalk outfits, and maybe even some different jewelry if you have some really exciting statement pieces. You may even end up with multiple pictures of the exact same outfit, but with different accessories on each one... that's great too! Mix-and-match away, catwalkin' it up for your extra pair of eyes and/or camera. Remember, you want a picture of each and every outfit!

After you've finished with your mix-and-match fashion show, reward yourself and your pal with a glass of wine or a bowl of ice cream.... hopefully you've been re-hanging everything as you went, so there isn't too much of a mess now, haha!

The next day — don't wait too long or you'll lose momentum! — go through all the photos on a computer and decide what you think about each outfit pairing. Does it work? Is it just kind of "meh"? Doing this on a computer rather than a phone makes it easier to see, and also allows you to compare outfits side-by-side for better perspective.

Pay attention: is any of your clothing a "one hit wonder," that you can only wear one way? This is a huge red flag that that piece doesn't belong in your Capsule Wardrobe... or that (going forward) you will need to slightly shift the direction of your wardrobe so that item *will* play better with the rest of your clothing.

Delete the photos of outfits you don't like, and **donate** any items of clothing you've now eliminated from your Capsule Wardrobe as a result of this whole process.

If you think it will be helpful, now is a good time to print or save the photos of the outfits that "work" to create a Look Book — I especially recommend doing this for looks that are outside of your normal habits, since you might not otherwise remember how good you looked and felt in them. However, this idea is mostly meant to serve as a helpful tool as you're transitioning into mix-and-matching, and working on getting out of an old style rut of two. A Look Book is definitely not absolutely necessary, since...

.... the goal of all this is *not* having to think about pairings! Once you finish your Capsule Wardrobe, (nearly) all elements should coordinate effortlessly with one another.

So, in a nutshell, if you're not feeling comfortable mixing and matching, or still are reaching for the same three combos and not utilizing all the other great stuff you own, creating a Look Book can allow you space to experiment with your self-expression. AND it can eliminate any one hit wonders lurking uncooperatively in your closet!

However, the Look Book is only ever meant to be a temporary tool, since eventually you will "graduate" to fully and effectively benefiting from your Capsule Wardrobe without needing that extra step.

Always remember that you are curating a collection of clothing that you enjoy, and that makes you feel confident and happy!

Freedom
without **limits**

IS JUST A WORD.

-Terry Pratchett

via Devastate Boredom

Chapter 8 - How many items belong in a Capsule Wardrobe? (the question we've all been avoiding!!)

There's a pretty big issue that I have been deftly, skillfully, cleverly avoiding the whole way through the book thus far... have you noticed? Has anybody noticed?

I haven't mentioned numbers once.

I haven't said, "Only have 35 items in your Capsule Wardrobe," or "A minimalist closet should contain no more than twenty hangers," or ANYTHING related to numbers.

That's because I think that the number of items in your closet has to be a personal choice based on your lifestyle... not something handed down prescriptively by someone who doesn't even know you.

However, the number choice does need to happen. You *will* need to decide how many items belong in your Capsule Wardrobe. That's because, in order for you to benefit from the wonders of a minimalist closet or a Capsule Wardrobe, you need to set limits for yourself.

A happy closet is one that reflects who you are, and is filled with things you enjoy wearing every day.

Be honest here for a minute — is it even possible for a wardrobe of 100+ items to contain only favorites? Even a "favorites only" wardrobe of 50+ items seems unlikely.

Though if you have one, depart in peace my child! And more power to you, you delightfully self-actualized clothes-horse, you…

My goal — and I think yours too, or why would you be reading this? — is to only wear clothing I love, and not to waste time or space on junky just-okay outfits.

If you'll permit me to get all profound on you for a minute… our days on this planet are limited, friends! I recently made a deliberate decision to no longer "save" stuff for special occasions, or leave it in my closet because I'm afraid it will get stained or torn. I want to enjoy the things I have, just like I want to make the most of each moment I have.

Why wait for a date night out? I wear my favorite dresses at home in the evening for dinner with my husband. I wore my favorite necklace almost constantly for three years, and I recently lost it. I'm not going to lie; I was really upset about the loss. But I would rather lose something I enjoy because I was making the most of it, than have it sit safely in my jewelry box and never see sunlight at all. If you're not using it, is there any point in owning it?

Points to ponder anyway… and your answers might be different than mine. But I choose to "use it up, spend it out" as Gretchen Rubin says, and I believe I am happier for it. And my Capsule Wardrobe helps me in this endeavor.

My Capsule Wardrobe keeps me future-focused and growing as a person!

You might raise your eyebrows at that statement, but it's true. Here's why.

Do you remember the size of the pre-minimalist-journey wardrobe I used to own, that I described earlier? I had TONS of clothes, a number of which were things I had bought in high school. One particular sweater even dated from middle school!

That wardrobe showcased about five different versions of me. There was "don't notice me" high school Sarah, quirky-college Sarah (you've already heard about her!), artsy just-out-of-college Sarah, insecure-professional Sarah, professionals-can-have-personality-too Sarah, and then on top of all that, there was the Now-Me. (I wouldn't dare try to categorize Now-Me... I'll try in a few years once there's an even more evolved version, and I have better perspective, ha!)

The wardrobe we all want is a living, thriving, curated collection... the wardrobe I had back then was a museum dedicated to the past. Is mausoleum a better word there? Ooh dramatic, I like it.

Nobody wants a mausoleum in their bedroom.

At least I don't! *shivers*

I have zero interest in keeping a museum in my closet, reminding me daily of the past. While I value my memories and realize that my past helped create Now-Me, I want my focus to continue to be on making the most of the time I have *right now*.

I want to look in my closet, see favorites that make me feel confident and happy in who I am RIGHT NOW, and go on with my day energized.

It is VERY easy for an ordinary, limit-less closet to turn into a museum.

Want to know why?

It's quite simply because we already own too much stuff. If you have 100+ items of clothing in your closet, many of those things probably only get worn once or twice a year, if that. Nothing ever wears out, which means there is no reason to get rid of anything. The ordinary closet becomes a museum all too easily, reflecting past yous, rather than serving as a functional wardrobe for Now-You.

If, on the other hand, you have chosen to have a limited number of clothing, a "minimalist closet," then it is highly likely that your clothing will wear out. And that is a good thing!

No risk of stale, forgotten mausoleums here! Hurray for wearing holes in your clothing! For loving them into faded-raggediness! Anyone see shades of *The Velveteen Rabbit* here? Perhaps the more our favorite clothing is given the opportunity to become worn and faded, the more "real" we wearers will become!

When you do succeed in wearing things out and it comes time to purchase new clothing to replace them, it can be with your Now-Me in mind… Which means that when you choose to have a limited amount of clothing, your wardrobe is able to constantly evolve to better match your current goals, environment, and growing sense of self.

So, knowing all that, it's up to you to pick the number that will make your closet happy, and keep it future-focused.

Maybe you go the drastic route -- "I will only own 20 items of clothing" you might shout, brandishing a hanger to the sky! Or maybe you decide to drop to a 50 item wardrobe right now, with the goal of whittling it down further over the next six months.

I can see the wheels in your head turning now! Mull it over, friend. Take your time!

A note about what should "count" in your wardrobe…. I've seen people online make stunning pronouncements about having a "10 item wardrobe" — but usually you will find in the fine print that the number doesn't include "t-shirts, jeans, shorts, workout clothing, clothes to wear while painting, sweaters, jackets, or pajamas" (what DOES it include, I'm wondering by the end...). I figure it is fair to view pajamas, workout clothes, and those *"Well duh, I'm going to need this"* items (which you have stowed separately from the rest of your clothes by now, right?) as their own separate categories, but pretty much everything else should "count" in your wardrobe!

Here's one last tip... if you're having trouble choosing a number, decide how often you think you *should be wearing* each item of clothing. I'm going to go out on a limb here and guess that you're probably not okay with storing clothes indefinitely without wearing them, which is what a lot of folks end up doing without meaning to... If you have 50 tops in your closet, it will take more than two months to cycle through wearing each of them. Does that sound like too much "down time" for your clothes to just be lounging around, doing nothing? If you have 25 tops you will end up wearing each about once a month, IF you're deliberate about it. Does that seem good to you, or will you decide that's still too many shirts? This all is 100% up to you, but keep in mind that if you pick a good charity, the clothing that is now vying for its chance on your back once every couple of months could really do somebody else some good!

All about me... you voyeur, you!

Maybe you're still waiting to hear how many items I currently have in *my* closet, hmmm? Countless purges, a blog series, and one ebook later, my minimalist Capsule Wardrobe IS finally finished. Hopefully it won't take quite so long for you, but I'm stubborn... and I was figuring it all out as I went. Fingers crossed this book can save you some time and effort!

In the very early stages of my journey I was working on getting rid of old and unwanted items without having a set "number goal" in mind. It felt like I was making progress, but in reality I was just barely chipping away at the mausoleum in my closet. I created a photo Look Book full of outfits I didn't actually like, because, without realizing it, I had skipped the step of identifying my own style! I had been reading about minimalism for years at that point, but right about then it started actually filtering through to my day-to-day life and refining the way I viewed both my clothes and my "stuff" in general. Then, as I shared earlier, I started playing with the idea of writing a Capsule Wardrobe series for my blog, and hammered out the steps I needed to take to find my own style. Things finally began to click!

At that point, I did officially "choose a number" and was able to exorcise most of the ghosts in my closet as a result. My goal was to be under 35 items in my "warm weather" Capsule Wardrobe; a number I chose at the time simply because it matched how many color-coordinated hangers were in the box I had bought — ha! It also happened to be a good number because it was less than what I already had (I was at about 48 summer items), but it wasn't so drastic as to feel overwhelming. I kept whittling it down by doing a one-in, two-out exchange... every time I added a new "favorite" to my closet, I had to get rid of two existing items. Which meant, among other things, that the new favorite had to be something really, really good!

As I started getting closer to my goal number (around 40 items), the two-out exchange started to become so painful (along the lines of "but I love ALL OF THESE") that I switched to the more straightforward "one-in, one-out" for new items. To get me the rest of the way to my goal number, I chose a few items that I loved, but that weren't fully maximized to mix-and-match with the rest of my Capsule Wardrobe, and resolved not to replace them when they wore out. Even before that happened, though, I was struck by several surprise revelations that specific things I had been considering favorites *weren't* any more. See why it's so important not to take it for granted that you know yourself? Our preferences shift all the time!

The final evolution of my Capsule Wardrobe, sometime after that, was prompted by another of these seemingly-small revelations, when I realized I don't actually like to wear cardigans – you know, those lightweight, button-down sweaters? And I had a ton of them, in all different colors! But I realized that I would actually rather wear a lightweight, long-sleeve top for those in-between, "might-get-chilly" times, than wear a cardigan on top of a tank or short sleeve top. And when I *do* wear a short sleeve top on a "might-get-chilly" kind of day, I would rather bring along a lightweight pullover (which can do double-duty as its own shirt at other times), in place of a cardigan. And I had thought I had my style all figured out before that! Silly cardigan-clad me...

Once I ditched the cardigans I was inspired to switch **from two separate seasonal capsules to one 55-item year-long approach to my wardrobe**, with more than half of the items consisting of lightweight stuff I can layer so that it fits any season. 20-ish things out of that number are more specifically for cold or warm weather, but the rest of it is easily layered and thus seasonally-flexible. I also have five heavy sweaters / dresses tucked away in the *"Well duh I'm going to need that"* section in my guest bedroom. If you think that sounds like cheating, it's not! I live "down South y'all" and I didn't end up wearing a single heavy sweater this whole last winter... but next winter, it's anybody's guess.

So, it comes down to this — your final number might be higher than mine, and your number might be lower. If you like the *idea* of continuing to whittle down your number but are having trouble because you have so many favorites (it's a good problem to have!), then try a "one-in, two-out" system, or maybe just resolve not to replace existing items as they wear out, until you arrive at your goal-number.

Your choice of number is up to you but it IS necessary to choose, if you truly want a minimalist, future-focused closet.

Fashions fade. Style is

eternal

-Yves Saint Laurent

via Devastate Boredom

Chapter 9 - Minimalism & the rest of your stuff

Shoes:

I should probably start with a quick disclaimer, since some ladies love shoes and might already be sweating a little in fear of what I'm about to say. I understand where you're coming from! One of my good friends has a whole wall in her closet dedicated to her shoes, and it is a glorious sight to behold… for her, her shoes are very much art on display in a gallery.

If that's the case for you too, you might not choose to include your shoe collection in your minimalist Capsule Wardrobe. And that's okay! It doesn't have to be a deal-breaker in your quest for greater closet simplicity. You can read all of what I'm about to say with an easy mind, because you are free to choose a different system for yourself, in this and in everything.

However, I am not particularly "a shoe lady." I mostly want my shoes to be pain-free, and to match my outfit or provide a fun pop of color. I very deliberately gave up wearing heels a few years ago, as they're terrible for the bone alignment in my feet (I'm genetically prone to bunions) as well as for my posture and back health (I also have scoliosis, oh woe is me!). So it is easy for me to choose to extend my minimalist philosophies into my shoe-wearing habits. If you have similar health concerns, or if you simply like the idea of only owning a limited number of shoes that mesh perfectly with the items in your curated closet, read on with enthusiasm!

Shoes Requirements for a Minimalist Capsule Wardrobe:

1. Casual comfy-walk-around shoes (think trips to the Botanical Garden, sightseeing, or running errands — Converse, Toms, Keds, etc)
2. Nicer but still casual shoes (think lunch with a friend or Casual Friday — Toms could still work here depending on your style, or moccasins, loafers, etc)
3. Good flats / heels (think a dinner date or a party)
4. Seasonal shoes (boots / sandals).
5. Bonus: A pair of trendy shoes, or a pair in one of your highlight colors

Also tucked away in your *"well duh I'm going to need that"* section are:

A. Work shoes, if you have specific style or function requirements for your job
B. Tennis / gym shoes
C. Flip-flops for the beach or pool
D. A pair or two of really dressy shoes for weddings / clubbing / fancy dinners / New Year's Eve / etc.

I suggest having a pair of trendy shoes or shoes in a highlight color (see #5) because we never want to feel "boxed in" by our Capsule Wardrobes! If you deliberately provide yourself with room to play, you're not likely to get bored. Just don't spend too much on trendy shoes, since they probably have a limited lifespan in your closet…. and don't keep them past their trendiness! Once you find yourself avoiding wearing them, donate or sell. The point is not to collect a museum of past styles, but to have a fluid collection of things you enjoy.

True confessions: For years I had a bad habit of buying shoes that didn't really fit. I wasn't taking the approach of "beauty is PAIN, darling!" — I just literally didn't know what to look / feel for in a pair of properly fitting shoes, and tended to buy ones that fit too snugly. When, about six months ago, I added some foot stretches into my fitness routine with the aim of improving my toe alignment, I came to startling realization. My feet were actually "meant" to be a full shoe size bigger than I had been wearing for more than fifteen years… oops! As a result, I had to donate nearly all of my existing shoes and start over. The five pairs of shoes I listed above really are serving me beautifully, and there is a lot more space in my closet now too. Win!

Purses:

When it comes to purses, all that is really NECESSARY in a minimalist closet is one casual bag and one nice one, and probably a dressy clutch in your *"well duh, I'm going to need that"* section. But if you're rebelling at that thought, remember that you're in charge of your closet; if purses are how you express yourself, then that's awesome. But only keep favorites! And don't fall into the trap of "saving" purses for a special occasion — **if you like them, use them regularly now!**

However, maybe you find the idea of only having two bags incredibly freeing. If that's the case, you might choose to make your casual purse a more affordable trendy option, so you can replace it often guilt-free. Or maybe you'll choose to splurge on two really amazing designer bags, and keep them for years. It's your choice!

True confessions: I actually do have more than two purses. I have a small crossbody bag I use generally, and a cute lightweight tote bag for occasions when I want to bring a pullover or a UPF sun jacket wherever I'm going. I also have the dressy clutch I mentioned before, tucked away… and a huge roomy black leather shoulder purse. And a red leather crossbody purse. And a mid-sized black leather crossbody bag. I acquired all three of these "additional" purses secondhand, but they are nice bags and have situational usefulness that I know will arise again in the future. So, I store all the smaller bags inside the biggest one, and hang onto them. Despite calling this a "confession," I don't actually think it's something to feel guilty about, or something that is at odds with my minimalist tendencies. If I got rid of these bags in the name of minimalism I'd very likely end up buying similar versions again in a year or two. In my estimation, hanging on to them and preventing those future purchases is a way of not just saving me money, but also reducing waste on our planet.

I know myself, so I tailor my system to meet my needs and priorities. That is exactly what you should do too!

If you accept anyone else's system as gospel, you will end up getting frustrated. I guarantee it!

If that does happen, it won't be your Capsule Wardrobe's fault. Think all your choices through with your own environment and needs in mind, and find a philosophy and a system that **works for you**.

Belts:

From a minimalist perspective, you probably only NEED one or two belts in your "family of neutrals" — maybe one dark and one light, depending on your color scheme. I also suggest having at least one belt in a highlight color, since a punchy belt can really make an otherwise neutral outfit pop. From there, tailor your belt collection based on whether or not you wear them. If you love belts, I think it is 100% fine to have more than three of them.

True confessions: I have a terrible time getting rid of belts! However, in the process of creating that first Look Book a couple of years ago, I realized that wide belts don't "work" on me. I'm not sure why, since I love how they look on other women, but they just don't feel right on me. Maybe I just don't like the "constricted" feeling of a wider belt — thank goodness

I don't live in an era of corsets! Based on that discovery, I was empowered to get rid of all of my wide belts in a single swoop.

But… I still have a ton of belts and I hardly ever wear most of them. I have them hung on a nifty belt hanger so they're all visible and ready to go, but I still mostly just wear a narrow black leather belt, a stretchy iridescent beaded belt, two medium-width belts in highlight colors (red and turquoise), and a couple of patterned cloth belts / sashes that I wear with jeans.

And now I'm going to make myself get rid of all the others.

If I can't remember what they look like from another room, they're clearly not favorites.

Thank you, dear reader, for helping me continue to progress my own Capsule Wardrobe this very moment!

Jewelry:

Jewelry in a minimalist Capsule Wardrobe should follow the two most important rules for clothes and shoes as well: 1) Only keep favorites and things you wear regularly, and 2) Try to vary the "looks" of any new acquisitions. The Konmari method is pretty effective with jewelry — start with your favorite piece, holding it in your hand and savoring the sense of joy it gives you. Then go on to the others, one at a time, and decide which of them also bring you joy, and which are just hanging around because they were gifts or a really amazing bargain.

Don't take up room in your jewelry box with slacker items you don't even like! All of your things should pay regular "rent" in joy and use, or out they go.

Don't forget, however, that you probably need to keep a few things in the *"well duh I'm going to need that"* category here too — interview-appropriate earrings, that super-dressy necklace you wear every year or two to weddings, etc.

Last consideration with jewelry — think about how you can incorporate your highlight colors, or maybe pull in different colors altogether for some visual contrast. A new necklace or pair of earrings can also be a great way to update your look, or to test out a new color you're wanting to add in to your wardrobe, without much trouble or expense.

True confessions: I love jewelry! Earrings, necklaces, bracelets, rings… all of it. I had a huge collection of jewelry before I began my minimalist journey, but I have really whittled it down to "favorites" only. I don't worry about a number here, but I do try to make sure I'm wearing all the things I own regularly. I realized yesterday that I haven't worn a particular necklace in months — which means I need to reevaluate. Is it still a favorite? Do I have other favorites that I will always choose to wear instead of that one? If so, I will probably choose to get rid of it or multi-purpose it.

"Multi-purpose it, how?" you might be asking.

- Bling out your car with a beaded necklace or pendant hanging from your rearview mirror! Think colorful, but obviously not valuable for this one.
- Use a larger necklace as a wall-hanging, or part of a gallery display. Drape it over the edge of a frame, or award it its own hook.
- Drape a long beaded necklace or a pretty chain around a lampshade, for a touch of whimsical enhancement.
- Hang a necklace in a window where it will catch the light.
- Wind up a necklace and wear it as a bracelet or even an anklet.

- Put pretty rings or earrings on display in a dish or tray in your living room.

There's no law that jewelry has to live in a box! There's lots of way it can "earn its keep" even if you no longer wear it regularly.

Scarves:

Scarves are a great addition to a minimalist Capsule Wardrobe because they are both utilitarian AND visually appealing. Cold-weather scarves keep you cozy, and warm-weather scarves can serve to protect your neck and décolleté from the sun, all while adding a dash of color to your outfit. Scarves are also a great way to get in on that trendy shade or pattern everyone is loving this season, without spending too much money and without having to make any drastic changes to the core of your carefully-curated closet.

The rule with scarves (like everything else…) — only keep favorites! Get rid of the obvious non-favorites, and test the rest. Put them all together in one easily accessible place, and then, each time you wear one, store it somewhere else… maybe add it to a new scarf hanger or create a artful display area with hooks on your wall. Whichever scarves are left untouched in the designated "starting place" at the end of the season have been proven de facto non-favorites and shouldn't be kept. Scarves you still like but don't wear can be multi-purposed as decorative touches — as a dresser / table runner, in / on a book case, draped over the top of a neutral curtain, used as "filler" inside a pretty jar or bowl, etc.

True confessions: I love scarves! As long as they are bringing you joy, don't worry about having… um… more than a few. However, do make sure to keep them displayed artistically in an accessible place, to maximize easy use and enjoyment.

To Summarize:

Shoes and accessories should be judged by the same minimalist standards as your clothes. Are they favorites? Do they mix-and-match well with different outfits? Everything you own should be earning its keep. No free rides here, stuff!

Accessories are the finishing touches, the sweet icing on your minimalist Capsule Wardrobe. You might opt for a few expensive, classic pieces, or you might stay trendy in this area of your look. It's your call! Adapt the system to work for you. Wear what makes you feel at ease in your own skin — whether that's your grandmother's heirloom locket, or designer shoes, or the latest scarf from Target — and you're sure to look amazing! After all, if I can get all "Orphan Annie" on you for a minute… you're never fully dressed without *confidence*! I know, I know, the song says "without a smile," but have you seen that kid? Take a lesson from Orphan-no-more Annie…

Lil' Orphan Annie's smile is cute, but it's her confidence that wins people over! As a result, she achieves the life of her dreams.

Shine

like
the whole universe

is yours.

-Rumi

Chapter 10 – Sample Capsule Wardrobes to inspire!

Okay, enough talk, am I right? It's time for some visuals.

You should be able to identify each Capsule Wardobe's family-of-neutrals AND highlight colors pretty quickly. Pay attention to the bases as well — the more bases you have, in varying silhouettes, the better off the wardrobe will be. Oh, and a couple of layering pieces on top (sweaters, blazers, vests, whatevs) will also help to increase the number of possible outfits, while simultaneously expanding the "seasonality" of your wardrobe.

This first collection doesn't have any top layering pieces at all, because I personally am not crazy about them… and this first wardrobe is based on my sense of style. *bats eyes*

Important Note: To see larger images in full color, type this link into any web browser and head over to my site! goo.gl/6sKuuk

Comfy, Creative, Urban Neo-Indie Chic

I call this…. (dramatic pause) **Comfy, Creative, Urban Neo-Indie Chic**. It is a summer-specific capsule at only 15 items (much smaller than is generally advisable for everyday life, but perfect for vacations or traveling), and can combine into 45 outfits. All of the tops can be worn with any of the bases, minus the red shirt with the red pants because I don't particularly want to look like a fire hydrant. Check it out for yourself:

So, this is what you're seeing —

Four bases in distinctly different colors and styles:

- Black layering maxi dress
- Striped layering maxi dress
- Red capris
- Black skinny jeans or jeggings

Eleven tops, in my family of neutrals and highlight colors only:

- 2 grey
- 4 white (one with red accents)
- 1 red
- 1 turquoise with red accents
- 3 black

SO EASY.

Mindless, in fact. I can reach in my closet and: 1- grab a base, 2- grab a top, 3- put clothes on body, 4- walk out door. DONE.

Note that I have chosen to have a larger number of neutral tops, to accommodate a bright highlight color base. This was a personal choice — I could just as easily have subbed in another neutral base, and had more highlight-color tops. However, I happen to like the red pants. Your wardrobe, your choices!

Here are five other sample wardrobes, in various color combinations and styles, to get your creative juices flowing.

Remember, to see larger images in full color, type goo.gl/6sKuuk into any browser and head over to my site!

The first collection showcases a three-season business casual wardrobe. Here we have 20 items, that will combine into 190+ outfits.

Bright & Fabulous Office Casual

Quick, look at the colors! You should be able to identify the color choices pretty easily.

If you said khaki, white, black, and grey, with highlight colors of turquoise, plum, and sky blue, **ding ding ding**, we have a winner! Note that I included one white blouse for flexibility: the rest of the wardrobe is quite colorful, and I wanted to be sure to provide for situations when a subtler look might be appropriate. Range of circumstances is always a priority!

Also, did you catch the number of potential outfits here?? 190+! If that is blowing you away a little bit, and/or you're bestowing this book with a highly skeptical gaze at the moment, let me break that down for you....

The five bases at the bottom of the chart can be paired with ALL TWELVE of the colorful tops. That gives us 60 outfits initially. Then we have the white blouse that can be paired with all the bases except the white cropped pants -- and you might even pull that off! I've seen some phenomenal white-on-white outfits lately... I'm just playing it conservative so you don't accuse me of cheating with my outfit-numbers here, ha! The white blouse pairings are another four outfits, bringing us to 64 outfits. Then we have our top layering pieces, the striped blazer and the black sweater, which together triple our number of potential outfits... leaving us with a grand total of 192 pairing options!

Did you notice, too, the big jump in outfit possibilities between this wardrobe and the last one? This one, the Bright and Fabulous Office Casual Capsule, has 20 items that combine into 190+ outfits. The Comfy Creative Urban Capsule had 15 pieces combining for 45 outfits. If we wanted to boost that number, we could either do it by adding bases – each new 100% mix-and-matchable base would add another 11 outfit options to our wardrobe – or by adding some layering pieces to wear on top. If we kept that first wardrobe as-is and simply added three layering pieces (maybe a lightweight sweater, a kicky vest, and a chambray button-down), we would suddenly have a wardrobe of 18 pieces that combine into 180+ outfit options. A balanced wardrobe is a beautifully flexible thing, my friends!

Next, a three-mild-seasons wardrobe. This sampler contains 20 items, that can combine into 140+ outfits.

DREAMY, BREEZY, BOHO CHIC CAPSULE WARDROBE INSPIRATION

via Devastate Boredom

You've already figured out the color scheme, right? The palette here is shades of grey (those dark bases are charcoal), white, and then the highlight colors blue and yellow.

Note that because I chose several white tops, I did not include any white bases... keeping your color choices centralized by category will help maximize your combinations, while avoiding the same-on-same-color "fire hydrant" issue of the very first wardrobe example... or the khaki, *khaki*, KHAKI problem that you'll see in the next wardrobe!

Here we have a winter-specific wardrobe for a climate with colder weather than mine… 19 items, combining into 75+ outfits.

Cozy Eclectic Winter Glam

I wasn't so strict with the color centralization for this wardrobe, and you can see the toll it takes on the number of possible outfits… khaki in my bases, tops, *and* layering pieces, white in both bases and tops, brown in both bases and layering… getting dressed with this Capsule Wardrobe would take considerably more thought than the others. Having options for 75+ outfits is still great, no question! But 19 items COULD have combined into an even larger number of outfits and provided us with a much more hassle-free dressing experience, had different selections been made. That is an important thing to keep in mind as you're shaping your wardrobe, but ultimately it is simply a matter of preference for you, the closet curator.

As a counterpoint to that last one, here is an example of a more rule-abiding winter Capsule Wardrobe, consisting of 24 items that combine into 250+ outfits.

Gorgeously Curvy Plus-Sized
WINTER CAPSULE WARDROBE

via Devastate Boredom

The colors in this closet are carefully segmented to allow for maximum (and beautifully mindless!) mix-and-matching:

- khaki and charcoal in the bases
- olive, burgundy, grey, and black in the tops
- white / cream for the layering pieces.

No overlapping colors = no headaches! This is the "purest" form of Capsule Wardrobe, at least according to my system, and pays off in a huge number of potential outfits with no muss, no fuss.

This last collection is a mostly-summer wardrobe that consists of 20 items, combining into 175+ outfits.

CLASSICALLY FEMININE "PREPPY" CAPSULE WARDROBE INSPIRATION

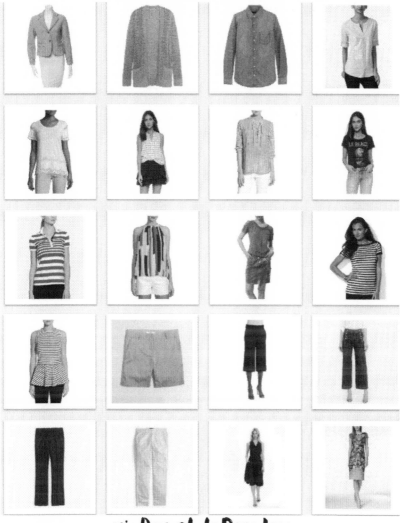

via Devastate Boredom

This closet is a good example of how to work a Capsule Wardrobe around some "favorites" that might not seem to fit at first glance – the pink-and-blue floral dress, halter top, and peplum top in particular. You can't layer the peplum or the halter top on either of the dresses, and the floral dress can pretty much only be worn with the sweater, blazer, or white button-down… maybe it could be dressed down with one of the other white tops too, but it certainly doesn't go with any of the striped shirts or casual tees. And that's okay! Because there are five other bases that balance beautifully with all the tops in this wardrobe AND three different top-layering pieces as well, we still have a plethora of outfit options. This Capsule also has the additional plus of servicing a larger range of circumstances than some of the other wardrobes we've looked at so far, since the floral dress, peplum top, and halter top can all serve important functions in dressier scenarios.

In the end, it's all about the personal style, needs, and environment of the wardrobe designer.

These are just a few sample capsule closets, for inspirational purposes only – it's not a bad thing if you don't see your own style preferences or favorite colors here. Honestly, I'd be surprised if you did! These are meant to get you thinking, and to help you visualize the possibilities for your own life.

If you'd like to see more, and maybe even peruse sample wardrobes with up-to-date shopping links for specific items, I've got you covered! Type this shortcut -- goo.gl/6RU02j -- into any web browser to find a growing library of sample Capsule Wardrobes on my blog, highlighting style suggestions for shoes and accessory choices too. They are perfect for jump-starting your own wardrobe search!

AND if you've looked all these ideas over and are still feeling uncertain as to what a capsule closet would look like for YOUR needs and preferences, come by my site for the scoop on my one-on-one virtual style consultation service. I KNOW that a Capsule Wardrobe is within reach for each one of you, and I would love the opportunity to help you figure out the details of yours! You can find details on that here: goo.gl/9NQeqs

But if you're already feeling good about your vision for your carefully-curated minimalist closet, then it's time to move on to the really fun part...

It's time to go shopping!

SHOPPING

is my cardio.

-CARRIE
BRADSHAW

Chapter 11 — How to curate your Capsule Wardrobe as you shop

Now that you have a Capsule Wardrobe, your shopping life is about to change. You're no longer going to be choosing new clothing haphazardly, or as a whim takes you. **You have a plan — a vision — a system. You're still going to shop, of course! But now you will shop with transformative purpose, guided by your insights into yourself and your closet.**

You'll resist buying that random shirt because you now realize that, if you did, it would be destined to live crammed into a drawer and neglected, only to be eventually freed from its unhappy sojourn in your dresser by a dribble of mustard the second time you managed to wear it... three or four years from now, maybe! You'll still happily browse the sale racks, but you will remain unswayed by the siren call of dresses too long / short / sheer / heavy for you — avoiding the toll they would have otherwise taken on your bank account and crowded closet. You will see the vast selection of the mall as an art gallery full of pieces you can admire without needing to buy, and you will test each purchase against the standards of "favorites."

And you WILL find more favorites, I guarantee it. If you're secretly worried that your Capsule Wardrobe spells the end of your career as a Mall Maven and Super Sale Shopper, don't be! You can continue to love to shop without impediment... you will, however, be more discerning now about what items actually come home in your shopping bag.

Ah yes, young Padawan, only three simple shopping rules there are! Follow them, and a Minimalist Fashion Jedi you will be!

Bonus "geek points" awarded if you read that last part in a Yoda voice…!

Three Simple Rules for Successful Capsule Shopping:

Rule 1 - "One-in, one-out."

I mentioned using this system earlier, but I'm bringing it up now because it can help SO much in keeping you calm and collected when faced with a really-ridiculously-good sale. If, in order to bring new things home, you have to get rid of an equal number of old things, you're guaranteed to keep improving the quality of your wardrobe as you carefully curate your collection of clothing over time. After all, if you're absolutely in love with all the tops you already own, that mostly-okay blouse dangling off the sales rack won't be able to bewitch you into an impulse buy you will later regret.

In addition, make sure that the item that is coming in "matches" the item that is going out. In other words, if you're buying a new neutral top, then the item you're getting rid of to make room for it should *also* be a neutral top. And if you're getting an item in a highlight color, a highlight color should also be what you discard, *not* a neutral. You should never get rid of a base to make room for a top, and vice versa! This method preserves the balance of your wardrobe, while allowing you to be flexible with new purchases.

Rule 2 - Stay strong and stick to your established colors.

At this point you might be screaming, "But you said I could switch out my highlight colors when I'm ready, you SAID so!"

And yes, you certainly can switch out your highlight colors whenever you want. In fact, as long as your new color "goes" with your existing bases AND layering colors AND accessories, you can add in a new color at any point pretty painlessly. However, if the new color you're flirting with is one that clashes with your existing pieces, then you're going to need to think that through and figure out a strategy for what you will need to replace in order to get your closet back to its fully mix-and-matchable glory in the near future.

And if your new color crush is super trendy at the moment but you're not necessarily sure you're going to want to make it a permanent part of your curated collection, then keep in mind what we discussed in the chapter on accessories — scarves, jewelry, etc, can be a great way to give your wardrobe a little fresh "oomph" without too much upheaval.

Rule 3 - Vary your silhouettes.

For now I'll just say that it can be dangerously easy to accidentally purchase things that are nearly identical to items of clothing you already own. I have some entertaining examples of this coming in Chapter 12! While you're shopping, look for variety in color and shape, and think flexibility in a range of circumstances.

Those are the Golden Rules of shopping for your curated closet, but here are a few additional general guidelines to keep in mind as well.

Guidelines for General Effective Shopping:

Guideline 1 - "If only" = don't buy it!

If something is just slightly "off," it's easy to end up thinking you can make it work. If you are standing there muttering "*If only* this shirt wasn't a little too big / small / short / long etc" then DO NOT BUY IT! Buying something that "almost works" is basically code for "I won't end up wearing or keeping this" and you might as well save your money for something better.

The one exception I would make in this type of scenario is if you need a "placeholder" item for your Capsule Wardrobe until you find a new favorite — it's fine to buy a less-than-perfect navy shirt, if you *know* you will wear that navy shirt until you find the perfect one. But again, if you won't wear something, there is no point in having it at all.

Guideline 2 - Go shopping for specific categories of things.

It is SO easy to get lost and overwhelmed in those racks and racks of different colors and brands and textures, and to lose sight of what will actually work in your closet. Have guidelines for yourself before you go into a store — "I'm looking for layering dresses in my family of neutrals" or "I'm looking for black shirts" or even just "I'm looking for tops in my highlight colors." This gives you a guiding "mission" for your shopping trip. You'll be less overwhelmed, and you'll be less likely to come home with something you don't really want.

The exception to this guideline, of course, is when you don't really "need" anything new, and are just shopping for fun. That can be the best kind of shopping! Wander, browse, and try-on freely, keeping in mind the "one-in, one-out," rule. Anything you buy should be enough of a new "favorite" that you will gladly get rid of an existing favorite to make way for it. Your closet is just going to keep getting better and better!

Guideline 3 – When shopping online, know your measurements.

If you're shopping online, be sure to know your measurements! As I'm sure you're already well aware, a medium in one brand is not the same as a medium in another.

The easiest way to approach this is to measure an equivalent item that fits, rather than trying to measure your own waist /

bust / etc. Also, remember not to limit your search too much — consider including the size above and below yours in your search parameters, since there can be so much variation in measurements between brands.

Also, be sure to consider the *length* of the item! That dress or shirt might be a lot shorter / longer than it looked in the photos, particularly if the model wearing it is actually 6 foot 3! Again, consider measuring an equivalent item with a length you like, to verify that the item you're shopping for will work for you.

Guideline 4 - When looking for specific items in specific colors, shopping online – and potentially secondhand – will be your best bet.

Once you have achieved a specific vision for what pieces you need to add to fill out your Capsule Wardrobe (a red skirt in a certain cut… a yellow button-down blouse… a pair of brown slacks, etc), then online shopping is going to be your friend, since store inventory will be much more limited to whatever color palette Pantone has decreed to be fashionable at the moment. In fact, you may discover that secondhand shopping is going to be your best bet for color choices that have been arbitrarily relegated to second-rate status this season.

I have had good luck finding specific pieces via eBay by setting up a standing search for the criteria of the item I'm looking for (brand, price, color, style, etc – maybe "grey J Crew pencil skirt size 12" or "teal Anthropologie top size small") and keeping an eye open for new items as they're listed. Online consignment sites like Thred-Up can also be great for earth-friendly bargain shopping, usually allowing you to tailor your searches by Capsule-Wardrobe-friendly specifics like color, cut, etc. Get on the mailing list and wait for a coupon code, and you'll get even more bang for your buck!

If secondhand shopping isn't in the cards for you, it's likely that you'll find yourself playing more of a "long game" with your Capsule Wardrobe – fleshing out and fine tuning your closet options gradually as your favorite colors and cuts cycle back into style / accessibility over the coming seasons.

As a sort of postscript on the topic of shopping, can I just say… please do not ever buy anything just because it is on a list! Whether it is "The 5 Styles You Need This Spring!" or "25 Wardrobe Staples Every Woman Should Own by 30" — these lists pretend to be one style fits all, and that is a cookie-cutter approach to fashion that is BORING! And remember, fashion "lists" of "must-haves" are designed to sell things. There is no cosmic imperative behind them, and, believe it or not, you can live happily and stylishly without ever owning a "little black dress," if you actually prefer chocolate brown or navy or bright colors instead.

On the flip side, don't be exasperated by what I'm saying right now if you actually find those kinds of "style lists" inspiring. Feel free to go to the store and try on the type of item that intrigued you — but then stop and consider honestly whether it will add to your Capsule Wardrobe in an exciting and functional way, or whether it will end up forgotten on the closet floor.

The bottom line: going forward, only buy new clothing if it qualifies as a "favorite" OR if it is a neutral or base that will allow you to wear your EXISTING favorites to better advantage.

MISTAKES
ARE THE *portals* OF
DISCOVERY.

-James Joyce

via Devastate Boredom

Chapter 12 — Common Capsule Wardrobe mistakes that will SABOTAGE your closet!

Have I mentioned I enjoy the *occasional* browse on Pinterest? *innocent*

In my time on Pinterest, I've started noticing a lot of clothing collections labeled "capsule wardrobes" that either 1) aren't one at all or 2) are making huge mistakes. In fact, it seems like some of the bloggers and fashion folks out there think that a capsule wardrobe is simply a specific number of pieces of clothing, that you've drawn a box around. Boxed in = capsule, right?

No! It isn't that at all. A Capsule Wardrobe is (say it with me now!) a collection of clothing specifically chosen so that *every item* can be worn with *as many other items as possible,* without the wearer getting bored. That can look different ways, but here are a couple of things is NOT.

Mistake 1 — Your wardrobe is monochromatic.

Okay, well, technically the black-and-white-and-grey-all-over wardrobes plastered across your Pinterest boards ARE Capsule Wardrobes, because they're very easily mixed-and-matched. But without highlight colors, they are BORING. Who, aside from a gorgeous *Paris Vogue* editor like Capucine Safyurtlu or Emmanuelle Alt, *really* only wants to wear black or white every day? If you try a monochromatic Capsule Wardrobe, I guarantee you're going to be bored out of your mind within a matter of weeks and you're going to revert to your previous, cluttered-closet, shopaholic self. Because, simply put, a bored wardrobe is not a happy one.

Pack that wardrobe with variety! Don't neglect your highlight colors.

Mistake 2 - Your wardrobe is very, incredibly tiny, because you have gotten rid of almost everything.

While you're certainly aware by now that I'm a firm believer in streamlining your wardrobe, there IS such a thing as going too tiny. I recently saw a "33 Items for a Year" wardrobe that looked completely impractical. It had 5 short sleeve shirts, 7 long sleeve shirts / sweaters, 8 bases (3 clearly only appropriate for summer), 5 coats / jackets, and 8 pairs of shoes. With 13 of the 33 items consisting of shoes and coats, that left a functional winter wardrobe of 7 tops and 5 bottoms — 12 items — which would have made 30 outfits IF every single thing "went" with everything else, which it didn't. **Even if you are currently convinced that an itty-bitty closet would work beautifully for you, think twice before making really radical cuts!**

Also, keep in mind — are you willing to do laundry frequently enough to keep your tiny wardrobe clean? I'm *willing in theory*, but I know myself — I'm just not organized enough to do laundry every four or five days. Once-a-week laundry is more my speed, so it is smarter for me to have at least a nine- or ten-day supply of shirts between me and "oh my God nothing is clean and I have work tomorrow!" Late night laundry done in a panic is never happy!

But aside from the laundry question, the more compelling issue is that whatever number of items of clothing you choose to keep in your wardrobe is going to have to cover you for the full range of "dressing situations" you will inevitably encounter in the course of your daily life. When I have offered scenarios of a 15-item wardrobe on my blog in the past, it was specifically *for one season* and specifically *tailored for maximum outfits* (usually around 45 possible outfits out of 15 items). When a person has a *severely* tiny wardrobe like the ones we're discussing, she will need to pick the content of her closet with even greater care than usual, in order to provide for the highest level of flexibility possible. It can be tricky to have that kind of foresight, especially when someone is in the first stages of shaping a Capsule Wardrobe anyway. I haven't seen any point in going that small with my own capsule, and I honestly wouldn't recommend it to most folks who weren't already experienced in the art of the happy, curated closet.

However, if you're over there muttering, "What is this writer-person even talking about? OF COURSE I'm ready to get rid of 68 items of clothing and have a 10-item wardrobe. Clearly she doesn't know me and I am READY," then try doing this…

Pick your ten items (or whatever very-tiny number you're so determined to choose) for your wardrobe as judiciously as you can, and balance your bases with special care! **Then, tuck away somewhere 10-20 flexible *PROBATION* items, that will encompass a wide range of weather needs, casual vs dressy events, etc.** I recommend hanging on to these things for at least a couple of months and maybe even a full season, to test your resolve about giving it all away…. and to test your ability to mix-and-match with the items you have left.

Because, while I don't usually suggest hanging on to "probation" items indefinitely…

…a really radical jump deserves a parachute! You know… just in case. *eyes ground warily*

If you have clear sailing with your super-tiny wardrobe, more power to you! You can donate that box at the end of the season without even opening it again. But if you realize you *do* need your parachute, it will be there, packed neatly away, and ready save your bacon for that work picnic, that unseasonably cold morning, or that last-minute dinner date.

Your Capsule Wardrobe is supposed to ultimately SAVE YOU MONEY (as well as hassle and headache), and I would hate to have that backfire in an expensive and very-headachy way because you got too excited and accidentally got rid of actually-quite-necessary-and-functional items.

Remember, you can always get rid of more stuff soon, if you realize your Capsule Wardrobe can do without it. But the Salvation Army isn't going to give that blazer back once you've parted with it. They're nice people and all, but they just won't!

A note about jackets, since they were included in the tiny wardrobe I described above — I would tend to put coats / jackets in the *"well duh I'm going to need that"* category, and not count them as part of my minimal wardrobe (along with pajamas and workout clothes, as we discussed earlier). In my opinion, a jacket / coat isn't really part of your outfit because, regardless of how cute it is, you're going to take it off when you get to your destination. There might be people who would disagree with me on that, particularly when it comes to lightweight jackets that work more like a cardigan, so I'll just leave that to your individual taste to decide.

Mistake 3 - Your wardrobe includes too many similar silhouettes!

I get to use the wardrobe above as an example again… remember those eight pairs of shoes? That wardrobe included a pair of Birkenstocks-type sandals, silver dressy sandals, a pair of tennis shoes, a pair of flats, two pairs of ankle boots, and two pairs of heeled "booties."

The problem here is that **there is too much similarity between several of the pairs of shoes owned**. As you can see below, the two pairs of ankle boots that were recommended both had dark colors and a similar shape — basically the same "silhouette," a word you will remember from the chapter on balancing your bases.

Too Similar!!

...vary your silhouettes.

You can see the same thing again with the booties, below.

They are quite similar in design to one another -- both featuring cut-outs and peep-toe -- and also similar in color, since one is brown and the other is light brown / tan. But let's go a level deeper, shall we? Take a moment to compare the "booties" and the "ankle boots." Is there anything keeping us from swapping the style names between the two sets of shoes? I'll talk more about this in a minute, but style names often serve to distract us from the fact that we are constantly duplicating our favorite styles in our closet… in this case, the blogger accidentally owns four very similar styles of shoes with a narrow range of utility and "look."

Do you notice something else about the colors involved in this "inadvertently sabotaged" Capsule Wardrobe? The designer has both brown and black in her wardrobe! And, as I warned earlier, it has resulted in doubling up on similar styles while limiting the outfit options available to her. Pick brown OR black as we discussed in Chapter 5, and you won't fall into this trap so easily!

Bottom line — remember to change up your silhouettes, in shoes as well as in clothing, to get more mileage out of your outfit "looks." Rather than buying a second pair of ankle boots, go with a pair of riding or moto boots. And rather than owning two pairs of high-heeled booties, go with one pair of booties and a pair of cute comfy flats that you can wear sightseeing in London, when you're going to end up walking eight miles over the course of the day.

Think about how your wardrobe can provide for flexibility and comfort in a range of circumstances, and avoid repeating looks you already own.

Here's another example of how people can unwittingly repeat the same looks in their Capsule Wardrobes — another blogger I came across posted a wardrobe that featured six bases. It included black leggings, black tights, a black pencil skirt, a pair of dark wash skinny jeans, a pair of light wash "boyfriend jeans," and a pair of light wash "joggers."

Maybe you're thinking, "That sounds good to me, lots of variety… what's the problem?"

Well, first off, black leggings and black tights both have the same exact "look." Even if there is a functional reason for having both (say, that the leggings are much warmer than the tights), the wardrobe "owner" would be wise to provide for more visual variety by swapping out the black leggings for grey ones, or the black tights for white. That tiny adjustment would provide a whole host of additional "looks" for this wardrobe.

The other big problem with this wardrobe scenario lies with the "joggers" and the "boyfriend jeans" is – well, here, see for yourself:

They look almost exactly the same! Despite having different "names," these two pairs of jeans have the same silhouette AND nearly identical color-tone as well. Not an effective use of bases for a Capsule Wardrobe at all!

It's pretty easy for this to happen, since we humans often gravitate towards repeating purchases of the things we like best. The fashion industry is also more than happy to assist us in this "style amnesia" by periodically giving different names to the same design, so that it seems new and fresh. Last season's knee-length "city shorts" are this season's "bermudas," and next season's "skimmer shorts." Each season, the fashion industry is just keeping its fingers crossed, hoping that our closets are too jam-packed for us to notice that we have now purchased three versions of the exact same thing!

So, when choosing items for your wardrobe, look past the name of the style! Yes, you like these "joggers," but have you already liked them (and purchased them) as "boyfriend jeans"? Stop and think - will the two items look basically interchangeable from 10 feet away? If so, pick something with more variation.

Steer clear of these three mistakes for smooth sailing to a yawn-free closet that mixes-and-matches effortlessly!

Style is very personal.

It has nothing to do with fashion.
Fashion is over quickly.

Style is
forever.

-Ralph Lauren

via Devastate Boredom

Chapter 13 — Organizing your Capsule Wardrobe: the world-transforming bewitchment of hanging "ALL THE THINGS"!

Now that you've developed a minimalist Capsule Wardrobe that reflects who you are, is unique to you, and makes you feel confident, it's time to chat about how to organize your clothing. While your closet or dresser probably already feels less cluttered just because there is less in there, organization is still an important element in the "effortlessly functional" aspect of your wardrobe. We want to store your clothing in a way that is easily accessible AND visually appealing… So let's dive into that!

There are a lot of blog posts bouncing around on Pinterest about how buying a matching set of hangers will **absolutely transform** your closet. So, I bought a set and tried it out.

Honestly, it really wasn't that revolutionary... still the same clothes, still the same closet. If you're relying on the "new hangers trick" to transform your closet with no other time or effort invested, you're bound to be disappointed. But since you and I have already invested a LOT of time and effort into transforming our closets (right?!), I have to say that the hangers were a nice touch, and helped my wardrobe feel "finished." So, as you read the following discussion on clothing storage, picture it with a snazzy set of matching hangers added to the bargain.

It's likely you've already heard of *The Life Changing Magic of Tidying Up,* by Japanese organizational expert Marie Kondo — her system of "tidying up" is heavily influenced by the philosophies of minimalism. Many of her suggestions won't be new to you if you're already familiar with the ideas behind the "simplicity living" movement, but Ms. Kondo also has some helpful approaches that are unique to her, and the book is well-worth a read.

Overall, I myself enjoyed *The Life Changing Magic of Tidying Up* and came away with some great new thoughts and perspectives, but… I strongly disagreed with Ms. Kondo on one thing. I COMPLETELY disagreed with her suggestions on the topic of clothing organization.

Ms Kondo recommends *avoiding* hanging clothing in the closet, in favor of folding everything and tucking it away in dressers instead. She even describes at length her precise method of folding each type of clothing. The idea of folding clothing a certain way and then arranging it vertically rather than piling it horizontally wasn't new to me; I came across a similar concept on Pinterest several years ago and have been using it to arrange my husband's jam-packed t-shirt drawer ever since. But that t-shirt drawer is the only place I find it helpful.

In fact, more and more over the past few years I have been choosing to hang things instead, to the point where the only clothes I store in drawers are my workout clothes and pajamas.

There are five reasons why this has happened; five reasons why I have evolved into hanging ALL of my clothing… and you might find there to be a good bit of world-altering bewitchment in that choice yourself, if you give it a try!

5 Reasons Why I Think You Should Hang "ALL THE THINGS"!

Reason 1 - Hanging your clothing displays your curated style collection, like the "art" it is.

My closet is a happy one; it represents aspects of my personality and makes me feel more confident in my own skin. This can be true whether your minimalist wardrobe features souvenir t-shirts that bring back happy memories, or silk blouses and power skirts. I've worked hard to find my style and hone my collection down until it is full of items I value... Why would I not want to have my wardrobe on display where I can see it?

Reason 2 - Hanging your clothing provides concrete limits to your wardrobe.

Based on previous experience, I can say that it is possible to stuff an impressive, almost unending, amount of clothing into a drawer. There are no clear boundaries to how many things you own when you have a dresser, or dresser + closet.

However, when you are choosing to hang your wardrobe, you simply match how many items you want to own with the number of hangers in your closet, and from that point on going forward there is a clear, physical boundary on the extent of your clothing collection. I've already shared with you that, during one of the stages of my Capsule Wardrobe journey, I purchased a set of 35 matching hangers. Whenever I bought a new item of clothing, I clearly had to get rid of an old one, or there wasn't a hanger for it. Now that I have a 55-piece yearlong capsule, I have a different color set of hangers for the fifteen-ish cold-weather items I own. When it gets warm enough that those things are no longer useful, I don't even have to think about which clothing needs to migrate out of the way… the hangers keep track for me.

Choosing to hang rather than fold provides simple, tangible limits on my wardrobe.

Reason 3 - Hanging your clothing enables easy wardrobe organization.

No need to paw through piles of fabric in your drawers looking for that certain black shirt, and rumpling all the other items around it in the process! No, when your wardrobe is hung in your closet, everything is easily visible at a glance. Even if you are folding your clothing with the precision required by Konmari methods and are able to easily "see" all your vertically stacked clothing, you're only really seeing a strip of fabric. I can tell you from experience (my husband's t-shirt drawer has NEVER been so interesting before!) that one black shirt looks a lot like all the others when all that is visible is an inch-wide section of fabric.

When you choose to hang your clothing, you can not only organize by type (bases together, short sleeve tops together, etc), but by color as well. That means that **all your clothing is literally accessible at a glance**. And that is SO lovely and easy.

Reason 4 - Hanging your clothing allows for effortless mix-and-match!

With dresser + closet, some of your clothing is in one place, and the rest is in the other. You have to keep in mind the items that are hidden away in drawers, as well as the items that are hanging within your closet, whenever you put together an outfit. We explored how you can create a Look Book to make this easier, OR you can just have your fully mixable wardrobe hanging in the closet. Reach in and grab a base, grab a top, and presto, you're done! If I have the momentary "what to wear?" hesitation, I can literally do just that... close my eyes, grab two pieces, and have an awesome outfit ready to go. And since nothing is lying buried in a drawer, there's no chance of a fabulous favorite piece lying forgotten and neglected.

Reason 5 - Hanging your clothing prevents wrinkles.

Marie Kondo argues that you can fold and arrange your clothing precisely enough to prevent wrinkling, but from my experiences with my husband's t-shirt drawer over the last couple of years, it's not quite that simple. In order for the folded clothing, arranged vertically, to STAY vertical, you have to keep the drawer at a fairly precise level of "filled." Otherwise the clothing topples over and *wrinkles like whoa* (that's the scientific term, of course!). This "whoa-like-wrinkling" can also occur if you pull out an item of clothing too quickly or carelessly, and the items on either side of it become dislodged as a result. Keeping your clothing folded in this manner, without having either wrinkle-inducing-scenario occur, would require rather meticulous handling and laundry-maintenance.

A further note on hanging things and laundry-maintenance.... I do not iron. I do not own an iron. I do not believe in ironing. In fact, I'm pretty sure that Moses just ran out of room for the eleventh commandment — "For the sake of thy sanity, thou shalt not iron." My strategy, in lieu of the despised ironing, is to either pull things out of the laundry still-warm and hang them, or to hang them up to dry in the first place. Either approach circumvents the need for ironing quite effectively, but when something already-clean ends up wrinkled (say, because it is stuffed into a drawer), I basically have to start over and re-wash it.

shakes head

Not worth the risk! So, I fold as little as possible.

For all five of these reasons, I highly recommend buying a set of hangers, hanging ALL of your clothes, and ordering them in your closet by color and type.

Of course, you can also hang everything on wire hangers and skip the purchase, but switching my clothes to the new hangers forced me to handle and reconsider every item of clothing in my wardrobe all over again, and provides a really nice visual boundary on how many items are in my closet. After all, if I felt like being sneaky it wouldn't be hard to find an extra wire hanger or two… it is much harder for my wardrobe to swell in number "accidentally" when I have matching turquoise velvet hangers to keep me honest!

Oh my, now that we've organized your closet we're nearing the end of this journey together! Just one last chapter *sob* -- but then I have a surprise for you!

Why fit in when you were BORN TO STAND OUT?

-Dr Seuss

Chapter 14 – A "Capsule Wardrobe Manifesto" (& farewell...)

We recognize our own beauty, and that each of us desires to be unique.

We choose to step away from the rat race of fast fashion, and the dictates of brands bent on making us buy more and more each season.

We reject the demands of an industry that regularly attempts to make us feel insecure about ourselves, in order to sell more clothing.

We choose to express ourselves through what we wear, and find our own individual, personal styles.

We find freedom in limitation, allowing ourselves greater mental space and creativity through fewer colors and items of clothing.

We glory in the contentment of a happy closet, adding only new pieces that bring us joy.

We are confident in who we are, and in the way our style expresses that!

Thank you so much for coming with me on this fantastic journey!

Together we've found your style, balanced your bases, made hard choices about color limits and how many items belong in your minimalist closet, donated and/or sold unwanted clothing, and began to curate your Capsule Wardrobe via your shopping habits going forward. You're excited about your happy, confident closet, and you're organized to boot! I applaud you!

applause

more applause

standing ovation

Seriously, breaking free of what our culture considers norms regarding clothing, material acquisitions, and "needs" is hard, and I'm so proud of you for taking steps in that direction. You're awesome!

I hope you've also had fun on this journey! Go forth empowered by what you decide to wear, regardless of whatever direction you choose to take your wardrobe from here. There are no wrong choices when it comes to your style!

Your closet and what you choose to do with it —capsule or otherwise — should be entirely a reflection of who you are, what you care about, and what makes you feel comfortable and confident.

Decide who you are, and BE THAT from now on. You are, and will continue to be, absolutely amazing.

So, own it! I'll be cheering for you over here the whole time.

Farewell, you gorgeous style-goddess you!

If you've enjoyed this book, be sure to sign up for more Capsule Wardrobe ideas and inspiration on my blog, Devastate Boredom! As a "thank you" for your subscription, I'll give you access to my library of free, printable, inspirational and motivational quote art, ready to be added to your walls and brighten your day. In addition to the style advice and fashion deal alerts you would expect on my site, you'll also find weekly funnies and frivolity, as well as book and movie reviews, life hacks and tips, and the occasional photo of my dogs, all courtesy of yours truly.

I have a tiny favor to ask of you, since you found this book engaging and helpful enough to read to this point… **will you pretty-please hop over to wherever you bought it and leave a review**? I would love to get the word out to the rest of the sisterhood of gorgeous ladies who are trying to figure out their style and curate their closets, and your review helps to do that. And happy karma comes around, yo! Just you wait and see…

In return for your review, I have a thank-you gift for you! I want to give you a little something special to remember me by, and to help you stay energized as you continue to fine-tune your style and wardrobe going forward… so, I've made the typographic quote-art found throughout this book into a bundle of free printables, just for you! Email me at saraheliza@devastateboredom.com and I'll get them right to you. These specific printables are only for my book-pals, and are not available for download via my blog, so you can feel extra special about that too, haha!

Drop me a line and say hi!
Your pal in style revolution, Sarah Eliza

Made in the USA
Columbia, SC
16 January 2018